Lefty Grove
and the 1931
Philadelphia Athletics

ALSO BY ROBERT P. BROADWATER
AND FROM MCFARLAND

*Civil War Medal of Honor Recipients:
A Complete Illustrated Record* (2012 [2007])

*American Generals of the Revolutionary War:
A Biographical Dictionary* (2012 [2007])

*The Battle of Perryville, 1862: Culmination of the
Failed Kentucky Campaign* (2011 [2005])

The Battle of Fair Oaks: Turning Point of McClellan (2011)

EDITED BY ROBERT P. BROADWATER

*Chickamauga, Andersonville, Fort Sumter and
Guard Duty at Home: Four Civil War Diaries
by Pennsylvania Soldiers* (2006)

Lefty Grove and the 1931 Philadelphia Athletics

ROBERT P. BROADWATER

McFarland & Company, Inc., Publishers
Jefferson, North Carolina

LIBRARY OF CONGRESS CATALOGUING-IN-PUBLICATION DATA

Broadwater, Robert P., 1958–
    Lefty Grove and the 1931 Philadelphia Athletics / Robert P. Broadwater.
        p.   cm.
    Includes bibliographical references and index.

    ISBN 978-0-7864-7566-7 (softcover : acid free paper) ∞
    ISBN 978-1-4766-1646-9 (ebook)

    1. Philadelphia Athletics (Baseball team)—History. 2. Grove, Lefty, 1900–1975. 3. Pitchers (Baseball)—United States.
4. Baseball players—United States. I. Title.
GV875.P44B76 2014
796.357092—dc23
[B]   2014018050

BRITISH LIBRARY CATALOGUING DATA ARE AVAILABLE

© 2014 Robert P. Broadwater. All rights reserved

No part of this book may be reproduced or transmitted in any form or by any means, electronic or mechanical, including photocopying or recording, or by any information storage and retrieval system, without permission in writing from the publisher.

On the cover: Pitcher Lefty Grove of the Philadelphia Athletics (National Baseball Hall of Fame Library, Cooperstown, New York)

Printed in the United States of America

McFarland & Company, Inc., Publishers
   Box 611, Jefferson, North Carolina 28640
     www.mcfarlandpub.com

To my grandchildren:

Kolby, the analytical child who delights in facts and statistics, absorbs information like a sponge, and LOVES baseball.

Quinn, the child of make-believe and superheroes who imagines the world in larger-than-life form.

Sophia, the child of wonder who looks upon life with unbounded joy and promise.

Acknowledgments

I would like to express my gratitude to the following for their invaluable assistance in providing their time and expertise during my research on Lefty Grove:

Richard and Sandra Grandstaff*

Deborah Hartman

The staff of the George's Creek Library, Lonaconing, Maryland

Your aid is only surpassed by the kindly and generous spirit in which it has been given.

*Sandra passed away on October 12, 2013. She will be greatly missed by her many friends, her family, and the numerous charities and organizations to which she so freely gave her time.

Table of Contents

Acknowledgments   vi
Preface   1
Introduction   5

ONE. The Building of a Dynasty   9
TWO. Another Run at Greatness   27
THREE. A Spring of Promise   48
FOUR. Seventeen Games in a Row   61
FIVE. The Boys of Summer   70
SIX. Dog Days and Another Winning Streak   92
SEVEN. The Drive to a Third Pennant   118
EIGHT. Facing the Cardinals Again   134
NINE. End of an Era   148

Epilogue   159
Appendix 1: Athletics 1931 Team and Individual Statistics   167
Appendix 2: Hall of Fame Players from the Golden Era (1925–1941)   171
Chapter Notes   175
Bibliography   179
Index   181

Preface

The Philadelphia Athletics served as the first dynasty franchise in Major League Baseball following the consolidation of the National and American leagues in 1901. In their first thirty years of existence, the Athletics, under the leadership of Connie Mack, reached eight World Series, and emerged victorious over the National League five times. With such stars as Eddie Plank, Home Run Baker, Chief Bender, Rube Waddell, and Eddie Collins, the early Athletics established a tradition of winning that made Philadelphia an American League town, despite the fact that the Phillies had represented the National League there for nearly two decades before the inception of the junior circuit. This tradition was passed on to the next generation of Athletics players, as new stars like Jimmie Foxx, Mickey Cochrane, Al Simmons, and Lefty Grove took up the banner and carried forward the winning ways of the franchise.

Indeed, this group of players formed the nucleus for what many baseball fans and historians consider to be one of the best teams ever to play the game. In the three-year period between 1929 and 1931, the Athletics won three consecutive American League pennants and two World Series championships. They dominated their own league, eclipsing the powerhouse New York Yankees, who had gone on the same run of three pennants and two championships, from 1926 to 1928. A comparison between the two squads ends in a virtual tie, with the possible edge going to the Athletics based on a somewhat better rotation of pitchers.

There is no question that the Athletics had the best pitcher in the game at the time of their three-year run, from 1929 to 1931. Robert "Lefty" Grove was the most dominant hurler of his era, and one of the most dominant of all time. There are many who believe him to be the

Preface

greatest pitcher to ever play the game, and many more who consider him to be the game's greatest left-handed hurler. It is certain that Grove was a major catalyst in the success of those championship teams, as he pitched his way to 79 wins from 1929 through 1931. The best season of his professional career took place in 1931, when he finished with a record of 31–4, leading the league in wins, ERA, and strikeouts, on his way to winning the American League Most Valuable Player award, the first ever given by the Baseball Writers Association of America.

Philadelphia also presented opposing pitchers with one of the most imposing lineups to ever step into the batter's box. Foxx, Simmons and Cochrane inspired the same sort of respect and fear on the pitcher's mound as Babe Ruth, Lou Gehrig and Bill Dickey did for the New York Yankees' famed Murderer's Row. Other star players like Mule Haas, Jimmy Dykes, and Bing Miller added timely hitting and occasional power to make the Athletics an offensive juggernaut capable of scoring runs in bunches and terrorizing starting rotations around the league. A well-balanced team, with both great bats and arms, Philadelphia stood on the threshold of passing from one of the greatest teams to ever play the game to becoming an all-time legend.

The Athletics opened the 1931 campaign as the undisputed class of the major leagues. They were the defending champions of the previous two seasons, and the odds-on favorite to win their third straight American League pennant. The team lived up to expectations by turning in a franchise-record season, posting 107 wins with only 45 losses. During the year, Philadelphia put together a streak of seventeen consecutive wins, as the team set a pace none of the other clubs in the American League could equal. Lefty Grove tied the American League record with sixteen consecutive wins. Grove served as the pitching ace on a team that boasted three twenty-game winners, as Connie Mack's boys seemed poised to become the first franchise in the major leagues to "three-peat" as World Series champions.

The present work chronicles the magic season when Philadelphia stood atop the baseball world as the game's first major dynasty. The book introduces the team from its inception, in 1901, and follows it through its tradition of winning that culminated in the three years of dominance, concluding with the 1931 season. In this golden age of baseball, when

Preface

Cobb, Hornsby and Ruth were household names, no franchise accomplished more than the Athletics. With a stable of superstar players in the prime years of their careers, there was no reason to think that Philadelphia would not continue to dominate the league for years to come. But 1931 was the final season the Athletics sat atop the baseball world. Plagued by financial problems stemming from the Great Depression, team ownership was forced to break up the powerhouse squad because ticket revenues could not underwrite the payroll for so many high-paid stars. The once-proud Athletics would spend the next two decades as the doormats of the American League, and would not return to greatness until the franchise moved to Oakland, California. In that city, the team would finally realize the goal of winning three consecutive World Series titles, as the A's once more rose to the top of the baseball world and experienced the thrill of dynasty.

As a young boy growing up in Salisbury, Pennsylvania, a small, rural town in the mountains of southwestern Pennsylvania, only a couple miles from the Maryland border, I was very familiar with the incredible career of Lefty Grove. Born and raised in nearby Lonaconing, Maryland, as was my grandfather, Darius H. Broadwater, Lefty was just about the most famous person ever to come out of that region, and was a local sports hero to many of the boys of my generation. Baseball and Lefty were a part of my youth, a cherished memory of innocence and simpler times, when summer days were spent with friends, playing the game we all loved, in most instances only ending when the light of day had vanished from the sky and the ball could no longer be seen. I continued to be an avid baseball fan as I entered into adulthood. The Pittsburgh Pirates were my team, and being a young adult in the 1970s was an exciting time to be a fan of the team and stars like Roberto Clemente, Willie Stargell, and Al Oliver. My favorite player, however, was Luke Walker, not surprisingly a feisty left-handed pitcher.

My love of the game continued until the last baseball strike, in 1994. The strike ended the regular season on August 12, and led to the cancellation of the postseason (the first time since 1904), as millionaires argued with billionaires over the institution of a salary cap and shared revenues. Something snapped in me as a result of the strike. In the years that followed, I found myself watching baseball less and less. In fact, the

Preface

only game I watched in its entirety was the one in which Cal Ripken, Jr. set the major league record for most consecutive games played.

In 2000, a miracle happened. My grandson, Kolby Cowher, was born. Like most young boys, Kolby developed a love of sports, especially baseball. His favorite team is the Pirates, and the devotion with which he follows every game makes me sad that the franchise has fallen on such hard times in almost two decades of futility. When I talk to Kolby about the glory days of the Pirates, I find that he can rattle off statistics about the favorite players of my youth with a knowledge born of passion and an unbridled love of the game. I also find that Kolby has given me a gift that I never expected. More to the point, he has restored a gift that I acquired several decades ago and somehow lost: a deep love for the game of baseball.

At the time I am writing this, the Pittsburgh Pirates have officially broken the twenty-year streak of consecutive losing seasons and returned to the playoffs in 2013. There is magic in baseball, as much today as in the era of Lefty Grove and his amazing Athletics.

Introduction

Robert Moses "Lefty" Grove was one of the most successful pitchers in baseball history. Widely thought to be among the best left-handed hurlers to ever take the mound, there are many that feel he was the best left-handed pitcher ever to play the game. Armed with a blazing fastball and a competitive temper to match, Grove earned 300 wins in the major leagues. Playing against the likes of Babe Ruth, Lou Gehrig, Ty Cobb, Mickey Cochrane, and a host of others, Grove was one of 41 American League players to be elected to the Baseball Hall of Fame from this golden era of the game. Grove is also credited with having the highest win-loss percentage in baseball history. For five years, he pitched for the Baltimore Orioles of the International League before joining the Philadelphia Athletics. Grove's record with the Orioles was 121–38, giving him a total professional career record of 421–179, for a .702 winning percentage.

In 1925, the legendary Connie Mack paid $100,600 to buy Grove's contract from the Baltimore Orioles, the highest amount ever paid for a ballplayer in history to that point. This amount beat the $100,000 that the New York Yankees had offered to acquire the great Babe Ruth from Boston, and was even more incredible when one considers that Grove, unlike Ruth, was not an everyday player, but a pitcher. Mack was in the process of building a team to compete with the Yankees for the American League pennant, and Grove proved to be the missing piece.

The deal did not pay immediate dividends for the Athletics, as Lefty went 10–12 in the 1925 season with an ERA of 4.75. The club finished in second place in the American League, behind the Washington Senators. The following year saw the big lefthander even his record at 13–13, while posting a league-leading 2.51 ERA. Despite Grove's improvement, the team slipped to third place, finishing the season behind the New York Yankees and Cleveland Indians. The 1927 season proved to be a disappointing year for the Athletics. Though the team finished the campaign with a record of 91–63, and Grove posted his first 20-game winning season and led the league in strikeouts, the Athletics finished in second place, a full 19 games behind the front-running Yankees. The 1928 slate witnessed the Athletics closing the gap between themselves and Babe Ruth's elusive Yankees. The team went 98–55 that year, and Grove led the league with 24 wins and 183 strikeouts. Nevertheless, the A's failed to win the pennant, finishing 2 1/2 games behind the Yanks.

But Grove and his teammates, which included Hall of Fame players like Al Simmons, Jimmie Foxx and Mickey Cochrane, were just beginning to come into their own. Grove had the third of his seven consecutive 20-game winning seasons, and led the league in ERA and strikeouts. In 1929, the Athletics captured the pennant by 18 games over the second-place Yankees, and defeated the Chicago Cubs four games to one in the World Series. With a team that rivaled the legendary Yankees, the Athletics repeated as American League champs the next two seasons. In 1930, the A's went 102–52, beating out the Washington Senators by eight games. Grove paced the pitching staff with his league-leading stats in wins (28), ERA (2.54), and strikeouts (209), while teammate and future Hall of Famer Al Simmons paced the offense with his league-leading .381 batting average. The A's met the St. Louis Cardinals in the Fall Classic that year, winning the World Series four games to two.

The 1931 season would be Lefty's best year in the majors. He posted a career-best and league-leading 31 wins, while compiling a league leading ERA of 2.06 and 175 strikeouts, leading to his choice as the first-ever American League Most Valuable Player. The A's captured the pennant again that year but fell to the Cardinals in a World Series rematch four games to three.

The 1931 season was the high-water mark for the Philadelphia Athletics, but Lefty Grove would continue to be a star in the major leagues. Over the course of his 17-year career, he led the league in ERA nine times, strikeouts five times, and win-loss percentage five times, earning him an induction to the Baseball Hall of Fame, as well as being named

Introduction

to The Sporting News list of "Baseball's Greatest Players" and the Major League Baseball All-Century Team.

The focus of this book is the 1931 season, during which Grove and his teammates established the high-water mark of the Athletics' success. Mickey Cochrane, Al Simmons and Jimmie Foxx turned in Hall of Fame careers by the time their playing days ended, but in 1931, they provided the nucleus of a fearsome lineup that posted a team batting average of .287 and rivaled the famed Murderer's Row of the New York Yankees. In that award-winning year, Grove was the ace of one of the best pitching staffs in baseball history while capturing the pitching triple crown and the American League MVP. Al Simmons won the American League batting title with an average of .390, with Mickey Cochrane batting .349 and Jimmie Foxx hitting a respectable .291 with 30 home runs.

A pitcher known for his fiery temper as much as for his blazing fastball, Grove hated to lose, and his tantrums following a loss became the sort of material that baseball writers loved to chronicle. Although Lefty was usually among the league leaders in most positive categories, he struggled with control. As a result, he was usually among the leader in walks issued, and was known to hit batters. This, combined with his disposition, made him a player that opposing fans loved to hate. Opposing ballparks were usually packed to capacity with cat-calling detractors of the perennial all-star. Lefty acquired a "bad boy" image around the league that only served to enhance and enlarge his reputation, and when he backed it up through such feats as striking out Babe Ruth, Lou Gehrig and Bob Meusel on ten pitches in the ninth inning to secure a one-run victory for the A's, it only cemented his legendary status. For this latest generation of baseball enthusiasts, I would like to introduce you to some of the all-time greats of the game. In the following pages, you will read about the end of an American League dynasty in Philadelphia and about the Athletics team that earned its place as one of the best ever in professional baseball.

ONE
The Building of a Dynasty

The Philadelphia Athletics came into existence in 1901 as one of the eight teams in the newly formed American League. The league was the brainchild of Bancroft Johnson and Charles Comiskey, and was formed largely from the old Western League. Johnson and Comiskey purchased the Western League in 1892, but financial difficulties forced it to cease operations on June 20, 1893, in the middle of the season. In November of that year, a meeting of Western League team owners was held in Detroit, Michigan, for the purpose of reorganizing the league for the 1894 season. Ban Johnson was elected league president, and he promised to bring fans into the fold by cleaning up the game and making it more appealing to the general public. Bad behavior by players would not be tolerated, and Johnson gave league umpires the authority to suspend any player using foul language or disputing calls.

Johnson's efforts to offer an entertaining but orderly version of baseball to the public was well received. In the league's first season under his direction attendance was strong, and the majority of the teams showed a profit. Attendance continued to climb through the 1895 season, and by 1896 the league was beginning to attract many high-caliber players and managers. One of the more notable converts was Cornelius McGillicuddy, better known as Connie Mack. An 11-year veteran of the National and Player's leagues, Mack was the player-manager of the Pittsburgh Pirates from 1894 to 1896.[1]

Following the conclusion of the 1896 season, Mack retired as a full-time player and accepted an offer from Henry Killilea to manage the Milwaukee Brewers of the Western League while occasionally serving as a backup catcher. For his services, Mack was paid a salary of $3,000 a year and given a 25 percent interest in the team.[2] Mack managed the

Brewers for four seasons, from 1897 through 1900, with his best campaign coming in the final year, when the club finished second in the Western League standings.

While managing the Brewers, Mack displayed an innate ability to recognize young talent and latent ability that would play a major role in his managerial career. During this time he discovered and signed George E. "Rube" Waddell, who was pitching for a semi-pro team in Pennsylvania. Waddell, an alcoholic who possibly suffered from a mental condition, had been cut by several teams because of his behavioral problems, but Mack would find a way to get the most out of his talent on the mound and put him solidly on a path that led to his induction into the Baseball Hall of Fame in 1946. Mack had a way of serving as a calming influence on his players. This ability would be tested a quarter-century later when Mack managed possibly the most fiery and most talented player of his managerial career.

In 1899, executives of the National League announced at the close of the season that they would be dropping Baltimore, Cleveland, Louisville, and Washington from the roster of major league cities the following year. The elimination of major league-caliber baseball in these cities presented an opportunity for Johnson and his associates, and they were not slow to act upon it. At the annual meeting of the Western League, held at the Great Northern Hotel in Chicago on October 11, 1899, it was proposed that the Western League place teams in all the cities vacated by the National League. The team's owners were more than willing to vote for acceptance of this move to the East. The National League had thoroughly entrenched itself in the most lucrative eastern markets, where it had monopolized professional baseball for years. Johnson and his associates viewed the placement of teams in the vacated cities as a golden chance to cut into the National League's dominance in the region. During that October meeting, it was also approved for the league to change its name. Beginning with the 1900 season, it would no longer be called the Western League. Since it was going to have teams in the East, as well as the West, team owners and executives agreed that the American League would be a more suitable name.[3]

During the 1900 season, the new American League continued to

ONE. *The Building of a Dynasty*

expand its fan base and offer a very enjoyable, family friendly style of baseball. Johnson, along with Charles Comiskey, decided that the time had come for the league to take another step toward competing with the National League. After the 1900 season concluded, Johnson convinced the owners in the American League that the time was right to form a major league to compete with the National League. Johnson pointed out that while attendance for the Western League teams had been increasing, the National League was experiencing a declining number of fans at the gate. The reason seemed simple to Johnson: the public appreciated the American League's style of baseball, with its well-managed teams and fan-friendly players.

After the owners' meeting, Johnson announced that the American League would be competing in the upcoming 1901 season as a major league circuit, on an equal status with the National League. Franchises were to be placed in Detroit, Buffalo, Philadelphia, Minneapolis, Indianapolis, Milwaukee, Cleveland, and Kansas City. At a January 28 meeting, before the season commenced, Boston, Chicago, Baltimore and Washington were substituted for Minneapolis, Indianapolis, Buffalo and Kansas City.[4] Johnson intended to challenge the National League's monopoly as a major league as well as its dominance in the eastern part of the country. In the cases of Chicago and Philadelphia, he sought to challenge the National League in cities where established teams were already located.

National League officials, along with most of the sportswriters in the country, dismissed Johnson's assertion that the American League would compete as a major league organization. The National League "has made a special provision for the American Association under its national agreement. The American Association will be known as a 'Special class,' a grade higher than Class A. This places the association on the same basis as the old American Association. Each club of the new league will be allowed every fall to reserve five players which shall be exempt from drafting. This, in itself, will eliminate all possibility of any drafting as no club carries over five players who would prove desirable in the National League company."[5]

But the National League officials underestimated Johnson and his new league. The American League would have a great deal more talent than was anticipated, and would from its start play a brand of baseball comparable to the National League. While the senior circuit announced that it had no plans to raid the players of the new upstart league, Johnson and his associates advocated a completely different strategy. The American League owners planned to actively recruit current National League players for their teams. More than 100 National League players were induced to jump ship and join the American League, including such stars and future Hall of Fame members as Jesse Burkett, Joe Kelley, Bobby Wallace, Nap Lajoie, and Elmer Flick.[6]

The primary reason for the defection of National League players was money. The senior circuit had established a salary cap for its players, setting $2,400 per year as the maximum that could be paid by any team for a player. American League owners were not constrained by this regulation, however, and offered salaries that in some cases were more than twice what the player could make under the National League salary cap system. Naturally, the National League cried foul and tried to block the players from signing with the American League through legal action. For the next two years, both sides were locked in a legal war that was ended only when the National League agreed to recognize the American League as an equal, following the conclusion of the 1902 season.

National League management had little choice in the matter. The American League teams were an instant sensation, and had quickly attracted a large fan base. In fact, the American League outpaced the National League in game attendance in both the 1901 and 1902 seasons, giving Ban Johnson and his associates the upper hand in their negotiations over the league's status. National League officials had initially hoped to incorporate the new teams into their league, but by the end of the 1902 season, many National League owners faced the prospect that their teams might be swallowed up by the American League. The agreement stipulated that each league would respect the player contracts of the other, meaning that the National League teams would be able to hold on to the star players still on their rosters. Johnson and Comiskey had done the impossible; they had not only created a viable new league, they had done so in such a manner as to threaten the very existence of the National League.

ONE. *The Building of a Dynasty*

The Philadelphia Athletics established themselves as one of the premier teams in the new American League. Johnson selected Connie Mack to be the manager for the new team, and advised him to contact Ben Shibe, a Philadelphia sporting goods manufacturer and minority owner of the Philadelphia Phillies, as a possible investor. Shibe agreed invest a 50 percent stake in the venture. Mack bought in for a 25 percent share, and the final 25 percent was divided between Philadelphia sportswriters Sam Jones and Frank Hough. The partners formed a corporation and drew up plans for their new team, but at this point, the Philadelphia Athletics existed in name alone. There was no team yet, and there was no place for the team to play once they recruited players to fill out the roster.

Mack began walking the streets of Philadelphia, searching for an appropriate site to build a ballpark. Time was running short before the 1901 season was due to commence, and for a while, Mack thought he might have to settle for a city park. Then, with about six weeks to go before the Athletics were to play their first game, Mack found a plot of ground at the corner of Twenty-ninth and Oxford streets that seemed to fit their needs. Shibe and Mack were able to negotiate a 10-year lease on the property, and with just five weeks remaining until the opening of the season, work was begun to construct stands around the field. In short order, a single-decked grandstand took form, and Columbia Park, the first home of the Philadelphia Athletics, came into existence.[7]

When it came to acquiring players for his team, Mack adopted the same tactics used by other American League owners: he raided the National League. A ready source of talent was right across town in the form of the Philadelphia Phillies. Mack was able to lure star second baseman Nap Lajoie away from the Phillies by offering him a salary of $6,000 a year, more than double his current pay. He also enticed pitchers Chick Fraser and Bill Bernhard to become part of his starting rotation, as well as shortstop Joe Dolan. Catcher Doc Baker, first baseman Harry Davis, third baseman Lave Cross, and outfielders Socks Seybold and Dave Fultz were all veterans of National League teams with proven ability. The only starting position player for the Athletics who had not played in the National League was rookie outfielder Matty McIntyre. Another promising rookie who would be making his debut with the team was Eddie

Plank, a starting pitcher Mack discovered at Gettysburg College who would eventually win more than 300 games in the majors, all of them with the Athletics, before being inducted into the Baseball Hall of Fame.[8] With this collection of proven talent, the Athletics embarked upon the inaugural 1901 season. While the club proved to be competitive and entertaining, by the season's end it had compiled a record of 74–64 and a fourth-place finish in the American League. Nap Lajoie emerged as the first true superstar of the American League, batting .426 while hitting 14 home runs and driving in 125.[9]

During the offseason, Mack and Shibe sought to expand upon the success of their first year by making a few changes to their lineup. Outfielder and future Hall of Famer Elmer Flick was acquired from the Phillies, along with pitcher Bill Duggleby. Hard-throwing righthander Rube Waddell also was added to the pitching staff. Always having an eye for new talent, Mack added a few pieces to the supporting cast, and as the 1902 season approached, it looked as if the Athletics had built a formidable team ready to compete for the pennant.

But the Phillies intended to have a say in the matter of Mack's roster. They filed suit to prevent Nap Lajoie from playing for the Athletics, winning a favorable ruling in the courts. The only problem was that the injunction was valid in the state of Pennsylvania alone. The ruling did not prevent Lajoie from playing for any other team or in any other state. Accordingly, Mack traded Lajoie to Cleveland rather than allow him to be sent back to the Phillies. Elmer Flick and Bill Bernhard were also included in the deal, as they had also come from the Phillies and it was anticipated that their cases might also be brought before the courts. The move meant that these three players could not play in Philadelphia when Cleveland came to town, but they could play in all other games scheduled by the Indians.[10]

In the 1902 season, Lave Cross paced the team with his .342 batting average while Socks Seybold belted 16 home runs. Pitchers Eddie Plank and Rube Waddell combined for a total of 44 wins while throwing 57 complete games. Attendance soared, almost doubling that of the 1901 season and finishing with more than 420,000 fans coming through the gates. By the end of the campaign, the Athletics had compiled a record of 83–53 and captured the American League pennant, finishing five

ONE. *The Building of a Dynasty*

games above the second-place St. Louis Browns. The team ranked second in the league in overall batting average and their pitchers placed first in strikeouts. During the offseason, negotiations with the National League established the first World Series to be played between the champions of the two leagues at the conclusion of the 1903 season. During this time, the Athletics had to be considered the favorites to represent the American League against their arch rivals in this first showdown between the leagues.

In 1902, the Athletics adopted a team emblem that would continue with the franchise for decades. John McGraw, manager of the New York Giants, had been asked what he thought of the Philadelphia Athletics. Referring to the lofty sums of money the team had been spending to acquire players, McGraw snorted, "White elephants! Mr. B.F. Shibe has a white elephant on his hands." Reporters jumped on McGraw's comment, and a cartoonist drew a picture of fans at Columbia Park feeding peanuts to elephants. Connie Mack also jumped on the statement. Instead of issuing any retaliatory remarks, however, he adopted a white elephant with a baseball as the team logo and had it added to all the players' uniforms.[11]

The 1903 season began with promise for the White Elephants of Philadelphia. Plank and Waddell anchored a starting rotation that had proven itself capable of winning games. A new addition to Mack's rotation of hurlers was Charles "Chief" Bender, a Chippewa Indian who had been discovered while playing at the Carlisle Indian School. Bender became a mainstay on the mound for the Athletics for more than a decade and earned 212 victories in his Hall of Fame career. Plank, Waddell and Bender would combine for 61 victories in this season with the rest of the pitching staff adding 14 wins, and the team ended the year with a record of 75–60. This earned the A's a second-place finish in the American League, but they were 14½ games behind the front-running Boston Americans.

In the 1904 season the American League expanded its schedule. Philadelphia ended play with a record of 81–70, good enough to finish fifth in the pennant race. The 1905 season saw Philadelphia return to a position of dominance in the American League. The team posted a record of 92–56, finishing two games in front of the Chicago White Sox.

Waddell, Plank and Bender led the way, combining for 69 wins. Waddell had 27 of those wins, best in the American League, and his 1.48 ERA and 287 strikeouts earned him the pitching triple crown for the season. In the World Series, the A's faced John McGraw and his New York Giants. Connie Mack's boys were not up to the challenge in the Fall Classic, however, as the Giants easily won the series four games to one. For the time being, John McGraw's opinion of the Athletics had been substantiated. That was about to change, however.

After the 1905 season, the Athletics suffered several years of disappointing finishes in the American League. The 1906 season was marred by injuries, as the team finished in fourth place with a record of

Shibe Park. Named for team owner Ben Shibe, this luxurious stadium was home to the Athletics during the glory days of the franchise, and served as the model for many of the new stadiums being built at the time.

ONE. *The Building of a Dynasty*

78–67. Mack's boys bounced back nicely the following year, challenging for the 1907 pennant until the final week of the season. Though they posted a respectable record of 88–57, the team finished 1½ games behind the front-running Detroit Tigers. The 1908 slate proved to be the worst season in the team's short history, as it dropped to sixth place in the American League and suffered its first losing season with a record of 68–85.

The 1909 campaign would be a banner year for the Philadelphia Athletics and set the stage for the team's first dynasty. Connie Mack and his boys moved that year from Columbia Park to Shibe Park, a brand new baseball stadium that had been built on a city block on Lehigh Avenue between Twentieth and Twenty-first streets. Ben Shibe had purchased the property in 1907 and contracted the firm of William Steele and Sons to construct a new ballpark there. Steele's engineers had experience with the new technology of steel reinforced concrete construction, and had designed and built the first skyscraper to be erected in Philadelphia. Steele's design for the park featured a façade in the French Renaissance style, boasting arches, vaultings, and Ionic pilasters. The grandstand walls were of red brick and terracotta and featured decorative baseball motifs. Large terracotta busts of Shibe and Mack were positioned above the main entrances to the park on Lehigh and Twenty-first Street.[12] It was a magnificent new park, among the finest in all of baseball, and the perfect setting in which to establish one of baseball's first dynasties.

The 1909 season proved to be a dramatic improvement over the previous year, as the team finished in second place with a record of 95–58, 3½ games behind Ty Cobb's pennant-winning Detroit Tigers. The team had rebounded nicely from its losing season in 1908, and its record, combined with the allure of the newly built Shibe Park, helped the Athletics draw almost 675,000 fans through the gates, which topped the American League attendance for the year. Along with star pitchers Plank and Bender, the team featured what many fans referred to as the "$100,000 Infield," with Stuffy McGinnis on first, future Hall of Famer Eddie Collins on second, Jack Barry at shortstop, and future Hall of Famer Frank "Home Run" Baker on third. The nickname came from the excellent fielding of these four players, not from the amount of money they were being paid. In fact, the combined salaries of the four members of the "$100,000 Infield" totaled less than $40,000. Plank and Bender paced the pitching staff with 19 and 18 wins, respectively, and rookie lefthander Eddie Krause went 18–8 with an ERA of 1.39. Though the team was disappointed at missing an opportunity for post-season play, Mack and Shibe had the pieces in place for the first dynasty in American League history.

The 1910 squad made short work of the rest of the American League, finishing with a record of 102–48, 14½ games in front of second-place New York. The team was paced by the franchise-high 31 victories of right-handed pitcher Jack Coombs and the .324 batting average of Eddie Collins. The team ranked first in the American League in the pitching statistics of ERA, shutouts, complete games, runs allowed, and strikeouts and in the offensive statistics of batting average, hits, and slugging percentage. Connie Mack's White Elephants had convincingly won their third pennant and earned their second trip to the World Series.

In the Fall Classic, the Athletics were pitted against the Chicago Cubs, who had also run away with the pennant in the National League, finishing with a record of 104–50. The Cubs also boasted a stellar infield, anchored by the Hall of Fame double-play trio of Joe Tinker, Johnny Evers and Frank Chance. Their pitching staff was led by Mordecai Brown, a veteran righthander who posted 25 victories in the 1910 campaign. Brown had lost most of his index finger and suffered significant damage to the other fingers on his right hand in a farming accident when he was a young boy. Despite this setback, he had become one of the best pitchers in the National League, and would put together a Hall of Fame career by the end of his playing days.

The series opened on October 17, with the first two games scheduled in Philadelphia at Shibe Park. The A's jumped out to an early lead in Game One, scoring two runs in the bottom of the second inning and adding another in their half of the third. That was all that Chief Bender needed, as he allowed only three hits and an unearned run in cruising to the 4–1 victory. In Game Two, the pitching matchup pitted the club's aces against one another, as Mordecai Brown and Jack Coombs took the mound. Neither hurler had his best stuff that day, as Coombs allowed three runs while managing to strand 14 Cubs base runners. Brown gave

ONE. *The Building of a Dynasty*

up 13 hits, culminating in a six-run seventh inning, however, and the Athletics went on to a 9–3 win.

Jack Coombs took the mound again two days later, on October 20, at West Side Grounds in Chicago. Each team scored a single run in its half of the first inning and added a pair of runs in its half of the second. Philadelphia then blew the game open by scoring five runs in the top of the third and adding four more in the top of the seventh. The A's won handily, 12–5, and Coombs earned his second victory of the series. Game Four, also in Chicago, pitted Brown against Chief Bender. The Cubs trailed, 3–2, in the bottom of the ninth inning when Frank Chance tripled to drive home the tying run and send the game to extra innings, where Chicago emerged victorious in the bottom of the tenth. Game Five featured a rematch of the Game Two pitching assignments, with Brown once more facing Coombs. Each pitcher allowed nine hits in the game, but Philadelphia was able to cluster several together to put five runs on the board in the top of the eighth inning on the way to a 7–2 victory. Coombs had notched three victories in the series, and Mack and Shibe had won the first baseball championship for the Athletics franchise.

The 1911 campaign opened with Philadelphia as the clear favorite to repeat as American League champions. Strong pitching, clean fielding, and timely hitting helped the team easily capture a second straight pennant with a record of 101–50, finishing 13.5 games in front of second-place Detroit. Coombs paced the pitching staff with a league-leading 28 wins, while Plank finished first in the circuit with 255 strikeouts. Eddie Collins batted a hefty .365, and Frank Baker led the league with 11 home runs while batting .334. The team's accomplishments earned the A's a second straight trip to the World Series to once more face John McGraw's powerhouse New York Giants.

The 1911 World Series schedule was arranged so that the games would alternate between the cities of New York and Philadelphia. The Giants, led by their star pitchers Christy Mathewson and Rube Marquard, would begin the series at home at the Polo Grounds on October 14, 1911. Matthewson faced Bender in a pitchers' duel that resulted in a 2–1 victory for the Giants. In Game Two, on October 16 at Shibe Park, Eddie Plank took the hill against Rube Marquard in another low-scoring game. Frank Baker hit a home run off Marquard, proving to be the margin of victory in a 3–1 win for Philadelphia.

The following day the series went back to the Polo Grounds, where Christy Mathewson faced off against Jack Coombs. In the best display of pitching in the series, the Giants took a 1–0 lead into the top of the ninth inning. But Frank Baker reached Mathewson for a long ball in the top of the frame, his second in as many days, and the game was sent into extra frames. For his accomplishment, Baker was dubbed with the nickname of "Home Run" Baker, and the sobriquet would stick with him the rest of his life. After a scoreless tenth inning, the A's plated two in the top of the eleventh. New York was able to respond with only a single run in their half of the inning, and Coombs emerged victorious with a 3–2 win. Game Four was played a week later, on October 24, at Shibe Park. Mathewson was once more on the mound for the Giants, opposed by Chief Bender. Though New York jumped out to a fast 2–0 lead in the top of the first, Connie Mack's team battled back with four runs in the fourth and fifth innings, posting a 4–2 win in the game and a 3–1 lead in the series.

The following day, the teams returned to New York for Game Five. Eddie Plank toed the rubber for the A's, while John McGraw handed the ball to Doc Crandall. The A's scored first, plating three runs in the top of the third, powered by a home run by Rube Oldring. Going into the bottom of the ninth, the Giants trailed, 3–1, with just three outs to go. McGraw's squad was able to push two runs across the plate, however, tying the game and sending the contest to extra innings for the second time in the series. In the bottom of the tenth, Larry Doyle scored from third on a sacrifice fly, and the Giants walked off with a 4–3 victory.

On October 26, the teams returned to Shibe Park for Game Six of the series. Chief Bender took the hill against Red Ames in what proved to be the most lopsided contest of the Fall Classic. The Giants jumped out to a 1–0 lead in their half of the first, but the rest of the game belonged to the white elephants. Philadelphia exploded for 13 runs, posting a 13–2 victory in the game and winning its second straight series. The A's had scored more than twice the number of runs the Giants had plated in the series, a feat that must have pleased team ownership in this rematch of the 1905 series.

ONE. *The Building of a Dynasty*

Despite a record of 90–62 and Home Run Baker leading the league in home runs and RBIs while batting .347, the A's failed to clinch the pennant in the 1912 season. In fact, the club finished in third place in the league, 15 games behind the front-running Boston Red Sox and one game behind the Washington Senators. Connie Mack felt his 1912 squad was one of the great all-time teams in baseball, only to be bested by "the greatest outfield baseball had known."[13] Mack was referring to the feared Red Sox trio of Harry Hooper, Tris Speaker, and Duffy Lewis. Boston faced the Giants in the Fall Classic, as John McGraw's team won yet another National League pennant. The Red Sox hosted their home games in the series in their newly constructed Fenway Park, and won the championship, four games to three.

In 1913, the Athletics posted a league-leading 96 victories, finishing six games in front of the Washington Senators and winning their third pennant in four years. Home Run Baker had his second straight season leading the league in home runs and RBIs, while Eddie Collins batted a hefty .345. Plank and Bender posted solid seasons, winning 18 and 21 games, respectively. John McGraw's Giants cruised to the 1913 National League pennant with a record of 101–51 and made their third consecutive trip to the World Series for a rubber game matchup against Connie Mack and the Athletics. McGraw hoped that his one-two punch of Mathewson and Marquard could pitch the Giants past the A's to capture New York's second title in five attempts.

The series opened on October 7 at the Polo Grounds with the same alternate field schedule that had been used in the previous meeting between the two clubs. Chief Bender opposed Rube Marquard in what should have been a pitchers' duel. But both hurlers were a little bit off their mark this day, each allowing the opposing team 11 hits. The A's hits proved to be more timely, specifically those of Home Run Baker, who hit a home run and drove in three while leading his team to a 6–4 victory. Game Two the following day pitted Christy Mathewson against Eddie Plank in a pitching duel at Shibe Park that has to rate among the finest ever to take place in the World Series. Inning after inning the two aces shut the door on the opposing batters, and by the end of the ninth frame the teams were still deadlocked, 0–0. The A's had a chance to win the game in the bottom of the ninth, but two runners were thrown out at home plate, sending the contest to extra innings. The Giants scored three in the top of the tenth. Mathewson singled in what proved to be the winning run, then retired the side in the bottom of the frame to secure the 3–0 victory.

On October 9, the pitching matchup at the Polo Grounds paired the A's 15-game winner Joe Bush against the Giants' 22-game winner Jeff Tesreau. Philadelphia got to Tesreau early, scoring five runs in the first two innings and went on to post an 8–2 win. The teams returned to Shibe Park on October 10 with the Athletics holding a 2–1 advantage in the series. Chief Bender opposed Al Demaree and seemed for a time to have the situation well in control. The A's plated six runs in the first five innings while Bender held the Giants scoreless. But the Giants mounted a late surge in the seventh and eighth innings, scoring five runs. Bender was able to shut the door in the ninth, however, and escaped with the 6–5 victory. Game Five featured a rematch of the pitchers that had turned in such a memorable performance in Game One. Christy Mathewson took the hill at home against Eddie Plank, but his scoreless inning streak was shattered when the Athletics scored a run in the top of the first and added two more in the top of the third. That was all the run support Plank needed, as he easily worked his way through the Giants' lineup, allowing just two hits and one run for a 3–1 victory. Connie Mack's club had captured its third championship in four years while John McGraw's Giants had lost its third consecutive World Series, the last team in major league history to do so.

Following the 1913 season, the Athletics were considered to be the first dynasty in Major League Baseball. With three championships in hand, they had won more titles than any other team since the inception of World Series play, and seemed poised to continue their run at the top of professional baseball. In what was becoming a habit, the team won the 1914 American League pennant with a record of 99–53, and was heavily favored in the World Series against the upstart Boston Braves. The Braves had already established themselves as one of the first miracle teams in baseball history by winning the right to represent the National League in the championship, but few thought their luck would sustain them against the mighty A's.

In July of 1914, the Braves found themselves in solid possession of

ONE. *The Building of a Dynasty*

last place in the league with a record of 26–40. But then the team caught fire. In its last 89 games the Braves posted a record of 70–19, as they gradually climbed the ladder to challenge for league dominance. By September 8, the Braves had passed John McGraw's Giants and took over first place in the National League. They would go on to win the pennant with a record of 94–59, 10.5 games ahead of New York. The team's resurgence was largely due to the efforts of pitchers Dick Rudolph, Bill James, and Lefty Tyler. Rudolph and James each won 26 games that season, and Tyler added 16 more to the total, as the Braves pitched their way to the championship. On the field, Boston's pedestrian lineup was led by future Hall of Fame members Johnny Evers and Rabbit Maranville.

Slightly more than a decade old, the World Series had captured the imagination of the American public for a game that was already

Team photograph of the 1914 American League champion Philadelphia Athletics. This team, containing such notables as Eddie Collins, Chief Bender, and Eddie Plank, had won three of the last four World Series titles, and stood atop the baseball world as the game's first dynasty. An unbelievable loss in the 1914 World Series to the upstart Boston Braves brought about a break up of the team, however, and witnessed a period of almost two decades before Philadelphia's return to dominance in the game.

ingrained as the national pastime. As most of the rest of the world focused its attention on the war raging in Europe, many people in the United States were fixated on the improbable matchup of Boston's unlikely winners against Philadelphia's series-tested champions.

The Athletics' roster of proven winners was filled with confidence when the team took the field at Shibe Park on October 9, 1914. Veteran Chief Bender took the mound to oppose Dick Rudolph. The Braves stepped out to an early lead in the contest when they scored two runs in the top of the second. Rudolph then took over the game, scattering five hits while striking out eight A's batters and allowing only one run. Boston, meanwhile, unleashed an offensive attack that accounted for eleven hits and seven runs. To add insult to injury, the Braves scored their final run in the top of the eighth inning by stealing home, and the Athletics were handed a defeat in Game One by the score of 7–1. Game Two was also played at Shibe Park, on October 10. Bill James and Eddie Plank locked in a pitchers' duel through eight innings. The A's bats went cold, as James allowed only two hits. In fact, in the first eight innings, the A's had only three base runners, and two of them were picked off by James. Plank scattered seven hits but managed to keep the Braves off the board until the top of the ninth. Charlie Deal doubled and then stole third before scoring on a two-out single by Les Mann. James shut the door in the bottom of the inning to secure a 1–0 victory in the game and a 2–0 lead for Boston in the series.

The upstart Braves had shocked Philadelphia by beating the Athletics in the first two games of the series in their home park. With the series now moving to Boston, it looked as if the impossible could come to pass; the mighty A's might lose this series. After a travel day, Game Three of the series was played at Fenway Park on October 12, 1914. The baseball world was treated to one of the best games ever to be played in the World Series. The Athletics sent lefthander Joe Bush to the mound against Lefty Tyler. Tyler turned in a gem of a pitching performance, but Bush was up to the challenge. At the end of nine innings the score was tied at two runs apiece. Philadelphia plated two runs in the top of the tenth, but Boston matched them in its half of the frame. After a scoreless eleventh, in which James was brought in to relieve Tyler, both teams moved to the twelfth. Philadelphia was blanked in their half of

ONE. *The Building of a Dynasty*

the inning. In the bottom of the frame, Bush found himself in trouble after giving up a double to Hank Gowdy. The next batter, Herbie Moran, attempted to move the runner to third with a bunt. Bush fielded the bunt and attempted to cut down the lead runner, but his throw to third sailed wildly, allowing Gowdy to scamper home with the winning run. The Braves were leading the series, 3–0, and on the verge of completing one of the most incredible upsets in sports.

In Game Four, Connie Mack sent lefthander Bob Shawkey to the mound to face Rudolph. The Braves broke on top with a run in the bottom of the fourth, but the Athletics answered with a run of their own in the top of the fifth. Johnny Evers drove in two runs with a single in the home half of the fifth, and that was the ball game. Rudolph frustrated the A's batters through the final innings, allowing just one base runner in the last four frames on the way to a 3–1 victory and a series sweep of the mighty Athletics. At least the humiliation did not take place in Philadelphia in front of their own fans, but then that was just a part of another streak the A's had put together. Thus far, they had been in five World Series, winning three and losing two. The final game of each series had been played in the opponent's ballpark, meaning A's fans did not have to deal with the humiliation of the 1914 collapse. They also had not gotten to celebrate any of the three victorious campaigns at home.

The failure of the Athletics to win their fourth World Series in five years signaled the end of the team's first dynasty, as a wholesale exodus of players occurred in Philadelphia. This stampede of White Elephants was not caused by locker room disputes or trouble with management, but was the result of the latest bidding war in professional baseball. The Federal League was started in 1913 by John T. Powers. The league did not abide by the National Agreement that Organized Baseball had put in place, and raided the talent of many National and American league teams by offering exorbitant contracts to their players. In 1914, Powers declared his teams to be a major league in much the same fashion Ban Johnson had in 1901.[14] The National and American league owners refused to enter into a bidding war to keep their players, and some of the top talent in both leagues defected to the new Federal League.

The Athletics were hit as hard as any team in baseball, losing several of their biggest stars. As Connie Mack put it, "The first to go were Bender and Plank. I didn't get a nickel for them. This was like being struck by a hurricane. Others followed. There was only one way to get out from under the catastrophe. I decided to sell out and start over again. When it became known that my players were for sale, the offers rolled into me. If the players were going to 'cash in' and leave me to hold the bag, there was nothing for me to do but to cash in too. So I sold the great Eddie Collins to the White Sox for $50,000 cash. I sold Home Run Baker to the Yankees. My shortstop, Jack Barry, told me he wanted to go to Boston, so I sold him to Boston for a song."

When asked why Mack didn't try to hold on to the players who had remained loyal to the team to serve as a foundation to build a new team around, the owner/manager responded by saying "that when a team starts to disintegrate it is like trying to plug up the hole in the dam to stop the flood. The boys who are left have lost their high spirits, and they want to go where they think the future looks brighter."[15] So the Athletics would start over. For the next ten years, the team suffered losing seasons, finishing in last place from 1915 to 1921. The 1916 squad set a milestone of sorts by finishing the season with a record of 36–117, for a winning percentage of .235, the worst posted in the major leagues throughout the twentieth century. The 1923 team finished 69–83 but climbed out of the cellar to finish sixth in the league. The 1924 squad improved to 71–81 and climbed a notch higher to finish in fifth place. Connie Mack was on the verge of putting together another A's team that would aspire to dynasty and challenge the mighty Murderer's Row of the New York Yankees as one of the best teams ever to play the game.

Two
Another Run at Greatness

By 1922, Connie Mack had bought out the team's stock owned by Sam Jones and Frank Hough to become a full partner with Ben Shibe. But when Shibe died that year his sons, Tom and John, assumed control of their father's interest in the team. The boys ran the business side of the operation, leaving the baseball side entirely in the competent hands of Mack, who had been busy scouting the college and minor league teams for talent. Mack was both a trend-setter and a nonconformist. He was the first to scour colleges and minor league fields in search of new players, and his success in finding talent caused the other teams to adopt aggressive scouting programs of their own. Mack approached the game with a business-like manner, and as such, he refused to conform to the universal policy of managers dressing in a baseball uniform. A business suit, tie, and hat served as his attire both on and off the field.

Baseball historian Bill James summed up Mack's managerial style by stating he favored a set lineup and did not generally platoon hitters; preferred young players to veterans and power hitters to those with high batting averages; did not often pinch-hit, use his bench players or sacrifice; believed in "big inning" offense rather than small ball; and very rarely issued an intentional walk.[1]

Mack's forte was finding talented players. Once they were brought into the A's system, they were taught the basics of playing winning baseball before being turned loose to go as far as their talents and abilities would take them. Mack believed in the old saying that players play and did not think that successful teams revolved around managerial strategy. Even so, he was one of the first in baseball to reposition his players in the field during a game based on the batter that was at the plate. During the last half of the 1920s, Mack discovered a great deal of talent that he was able to bring into the A's organization. By 1924, the team had turned the corner, and over the next few years players were added that would lead the A's to the top of the baseball world once again.

In 1924, Jimmy Dykes, Bing Miller, and Rube Walberg were joined by Max Bishop and Al Simmons. The 1925 team saw the addition of Robert M. "Lefty" Grove, Gordon S. "Mickey" Cochrane, and Jimmie Foxx. These three players, along with Simmons, would serve as the foundation upon which Mack would build his latest dynasty.

Grove was a hard-throwing lefthander from Lonaconing, Maryland, who had already amassed 109 wins in professional baseball and lost only 36 while playing for the Baltimore Orioles of the International League. Grove had joined the Orioles in 1920 and was a major factor in the team playing in the minor league championship series from 1920 through 1924. The 6'3" hurler had earned a reputation for having a temper as hot as his blazing fastball, which one sportswriter said was so quick that he "could throw a lamb chop past a wolf."[2] A hard-nosed competitor with a fastball as quick as anyone could remember seeing, Grove was also a workhorse who ate up innings. He once pitched six times in a single week for the Orioles. Grove's talent promised to make him a star, while his temperament assured that he would be among the players opposing fans most loved to hate. One fellow player described Grove's intensity and competitive drive by stating that on days Lefty was scheduled to pitch, he "snarled at writers, ignored his teammates, seemed to hate humanity."[3]

In his time with Baltimore, Lefty had already become famous for tantrums that resulted in the destruction of chairs, water coolers, and most anything else that came in his path as he vented his frustration over a loss. Those who knew him better felt that his outbursts of temper resulted from shyness or feelings of inferiority. Lefty had quit school at a young age and had not completed his education. As one observer put it, "I think he felt inadequate around some of the other ball players with a good education. I think he was bashful and ill at ease around people who could maybe talk a little better." The people of Lonaconing who knew him throughout his life described him as being kind, polite, and generous in all his dealings off the baseball diamond.[4] Whether his out-

Two. *Another Run at Greatness*

Connie Mack. As manager of the Philadelphia Athletics, Mack set the all-time mark for years managing, wins, and losses, records that will probably never be broken. During two different periods of dynasty, he put together teams that set the standard for excellence in the American League, and established the Philadelphia Athletics as the class of the baseball world.

bursts came from feelings of inadequacy or not, it is certain that Grove was a fiery competitor who hated to lose.

Whatever the flaws in Grove's personality may have been, Mack decided to purchase his contract from Jack Dunn, owner of the Orioles. Dunn had offered Mack the contract to Babe Ruth some years before but the manager of the Athletics had passed on the deal, and Ruth ended up with the Boston Red Sox. In 1919, the New York Yankees purchased Ruth's contract for the sum of $100,000, at the time a record amount to be paid for a baseball player. Dunn informed Mack that he wanted $100,600 for Grove's contract, an amount that would make Grove the highest priced player in history, to that point. Mack cringed over the money but decided to complete the deal. Attendance had been up at Shibe Park the last couple of years and Mack hoped the increased gate revenue would help to pay for his investment. Mack knew that Grove could be a star in the league and develop into the anchor of his pitching staff for years to come. And he hoped with his huge investment that day would come sooner rather than later.

Mickey Cochrane was another high-priced addition to the team, though his contract cost the Athletics only half what they had spent to acquire Grove. The 22-year-old catcher had attended Boston University, where he played five sports. His first love and the sport he considered himself to be the best at was football. He could make more money playing baseball so he signed a contract with the Portland Beavers of the Pacific Coast League in 1924. Mack was impressed with the hard-hitting catcher, even though his abilities behind the plate left something to be desired. Cy Perkins, the starting catcher for the Athletics, considered to be one of the best defensive receivers in the league, could groom the young backstop and teach him some of the finer points of calling games and handling pitchers. Cochrane would need some coaching behind the plate, but Mack was sure that his talent and ability would make him a star. The Athletics paid $50,000 to acquire Cochrane's contract from the Beavers, and Mack was so intent on having the deal go through that he bought controlling interest in the Portland team to ensure its acceptance.

Jimmie Foxx was another of the trio of future superstars that was added to the team in 1925. Like Grove, Foxx had been born in Mary-

Two. Another Run at Greatness

land. He had dropped out of high school early to sign with a minor league team managed by Frank "Home Run" Baker, and when Baker realized what the kid could do, he quickly got in touch with Connie Mack. The Athletics picked up Foxx's contract for a song compared to what they had paid for Grove and Cochrane, and the seventeen-year-old slugger was signed to a major league deal with Philadelphia. Mack planned to bring the young man along slowly, giving him spot duty at first base, in the outfield, and behind home plate. Before long, however, Foxx's ability with the bat would demand that a starting position be obtained for him. But in 1925, he was simply the fresh-faced kid who was long on talent and potential but short on experience and grooming.

The 1925 squad showed marked improvement over the previous season, finishing the year with a record of 88–64, good enough to earn them second place behind the front-running Washington Senators. Lefty Grove's debut season was less than stellar, and he finished the year with a record of 10–12, the only time in his major league career he would lose more games than he won. His 4.75 ERA was influenced greatly by the fact that he issued 131 walks during the season, the most in the league. He also struck out 116 batters to lead the league in that category, the first of seven consecutive seasons he would top the American League in strikeouts.[5]

Mickey Cochrane proved to be an instant success, batting .331 in 134 games. Cochrane got his first shot at fame when he was called upon to pinch-hit for Cy Perkins in the first game of the season. In the eighth inning of a tie contest with the winning run on base, Mack told Cochrane to grab a bat and hit for Perkins. Cochrane promptly rapped a solid single that brought home the winning run, and Perkins was heard to remark, "There goes Perkins' job on that base hit." His prediction came true, as he caught in only 58 games that season.[6] Cochrane was already on his way to making Perkins a back-up catcher for the Athletics. Jimmie Foxx got only nine at-bats during the 1925 campaign but made the most of his plate appearances, rapping out six hits for a .667 batting average. Al Simmons led the team with his .387 batting average and 24 home runs, Jimmy Dykes hit for a .323 average, Bing Miller batted .319, and Max Bishop hit a respectable .280. The team's offensive capabilities meant they were never really out of any game, no matter what the score, and their occasional outbursts of scoring gave the baseball world a glimpse of greatness to come.

On June 15, 1925, the Athletics were playing the Cleveland Indians at Shibe Park and found themselves trailing the Tribe, 15–4, going into their half of the eighth inning. Cleveland's starting pitcher, Jake Miller, gave up three runs while getting only one out before giving way to reliever By Speece. Speece was unable to record an out by the time Philadelphia had touched him for four more runs, and he had to hand the ball off to Carl Yowell. Yowell's fate was no better than Speece's, as he surrendered two more runs without getting a single Athletic out. By this point the score was 15–13, and the A's looked like they were about to pull off the impossible. George Uhle took the mound for the Indians and attempted to put out the fire. Uhle did get the final two outs of the frame, but he also gave up four more runs, and by the time the smoke cleared, the Athletics had come all the way back to take a 17–15 lead. It was the greatest comeback in the history of baseball, and the offensive outburst shocked the baseball world.[7]

The 1926 club featured the pitching of Howard Ehmke, a 32-year-old righthander Mack had acquired from the Boston Red Sox in a trade during the season. Ehmke, a 6'3" veteran who relied more on his off-speed stuff than his fastball, went 12–4 for the A's in the second half of the year, helping to keep the team in the pennant hunt. Lefty Grove improved his record from the previous year to 13–13, and he made huge improvements in other areas, finishing with a league-leading ERA of 2.51, pacing the circuit with 194 strikeouts, and giving up only 75 percent of the bases on balls he had the year before. Grove seemed poised to take the final step toward stardom, as all of the pieces started to fall into place for him. Al Simmons led the team in batting with a .341 average, Mickey Cochrane played in 120 games and hit a respectable .273, while Jimmie Foxx had only 32 at-bats but finished with a .313 average. In the end, the team posted a record of 87–63, dropping to third place in the league behind New York and Cleveland, but the A's were only six games out of first place.

During the 1927 campaign Mack added some veteran star power to the lineup. Eddie Collins was back with the team, and Mack picked

Two. Another Run at Greatness

up outfielders Ty Cobb and Zack Wheat to add veteran leadership and show his young kids how to win. Collins and Cobb were both 40 years old and Wheat was 39, but Mack knew they could still play the game. Cobb batted a hefty .357 during the year while playing in the most games of any starter on the roster. Collins and Wheat saw more limited playing time; Collins got into 95 games and Wheat appeared in 88, but they made the most of their at-bats and finished with averages of .336 and .324, respectively. Simmons once more led the team in batting with a torrid .392 average. Cochrane had his best year yet, hitting .338 and belting 12 home runs, and Foxx saw more playing time, getting 130 at-bats and hitting .323.

The greatest improvement for the Athletics came from their pitchers. Lefty Grove had come into his own. He finished with a record of 20–13 with nine saves, and though his ERA edged up from the previous year to 3.19, he cut down on his walks by 25 percent and led the league once more in strikeouts. To many baseball historians, this was the year that Lefty Grove finally learned how to pitch. Connie Mack had prevailed upon Grove that he was throwing too quickly and not taking time to aim his pitches. Mack got Lefty to slow down his delivery by having him count to ten after getting the ball from the catcher. By being more deliberate, Grove was able to control his wildness and cut down significantly on the number of walks he allowed. His famed fastball, which one former player described as being "four or five inches higher than you thought it was, which made the players think it was jumping, but it wasn't jumping. It came so fast it created an illusion," was now under control, making Lefty all the harder to hit.[8] It was the beginning of a seven-year stretch where Grove would become the most dominant pitcher in the game. Walberg added 16 victories to the total, Jack Quinn won 15, and Ehmke kicked in 12.

The A's finished the campaign with a record of 91–63. Some years that mark would have been good enough to capture the pennant, but not in 1927. That was the year of Murderer's Row, the famed New York Yankee team of manager Miller Huggins, featuring Babe Ruth, Lou Gehrig, Tony Lazzeri, Earle Combs, Bob Meusel, Waite Hoyt, and Herb Pennock. The Yankees won 110 games that season while running away with the title. Connie Mack had gotten his A's back into winning form as one of the best teams in the league, but he needed to find a way to jump over the powerful Yankees if he wanted to win another pennant for Philadelphia.

Mack added three new faces to the lineup for the 1928 season while eliminating one iconic logo. Beginning in 1928, the white elephant logo was removed from the uniforms of A's players.[9] Tris Speaker, the 40-year-old future Hall of Fame outfielder, was signed to replace the departed Zack Wheat. Mack went back to Baltimore to purchase the contract of 28-year-old George "Moose" Earnshaw, a 6'4" right-handed fireballer Connie felt could add a little zip to his starting rotation. Neither addition panned out particularly well for the 1928 season. Speaker had an off-year, batting only .267 in limited play. He would hang up his spikes at the conclusion of the season, calling it a career. Ty Cobb got the last 114 hits of his career, batting .323 for the season before announcing his retirement. The rookie Earnshaw went 7–7 with an ERA of 3.81. Speaker's and Cobb's careers were ending, but Earnshaw's was just getting started. Over the next few seasons he would become a mainstay on the mound, a right-handed complement to Grove's left-handed heat. George "Mule" Haas was a 24-year-old rookie whose contract the A's purchased from the minor leagues. The 6'1" left-handed batter would get into 91 games in 1928 and finish with a respectable .280 batting average. Along with Earnshaw, Haas was destined to become an integral part of the Athletics' future. Simmons continued to lead the team in hitting, batting .351 while swatting 15 home runs. Cochrane's average slipped to a still-respectable .293, and Foxx became a starter, at last, taking over the first base duties and hitting .328. In the 1928 campaign, Foxx first showed the signs of power that would define his Hall of Fame career by belting 13 home runs. Lefty Grove posted his best record yet at 24–8 with a 2.58 ERA. His 24 wins were the best in the American League, and he led the circuit in strikeouts for the fourth consecutive year with 183. The team finished the season with a record of 98–55, and battled the Yankees all year for the top spot.

On September 8, the A's were in first place with a half-game lead over the Yankees. The following day the team traveled to New York to open a four-game series against their archrivals. The Yankees took three of the four games, breaking Lefty Grove's 14-game winning streak in the

TWO. *Another Run at Greatness*

process. The A's limped out of New York 1½ games back in the standings, and though they continued to keep the heat on the Yanks for the remainder of the season, they finished the campaign 2½ games back of the Bronx pinstripers.[10]

By the beginning of the 1929 season the Philadelphia Athletics were poised to once more move to the forefront as one of the best teams in baseball. But only the members of the A's organization and their fans believed this to be true. To the rest of the baseball world, the Yankees seemed invincible. They had won consecutive World Series titles and were the odds-on favorite to make it three in a row. Most players and fans outside of Philadelphia considered the Athletics to be a great team but a notch below the Yankees. Miller Huggins, the skipper of the Yankees, seemed confident about his team's ability to three-peat when he stated in spring training, "Now don't quote me as saying the Yanks will cop another pennant. What I will say is that we seem to have pennant power. I have confidence in the team, like their spirit, and see no signs

The 1929 Philadelphia Athletics. With stars like Grove, Foxx, Simmons, and Cochrane, the 1929 squad powered its way past the New York Yankees to win the pennant before beating the Chicago Cubs in the World Series. The Athletics were back on top, and from 1929–1931 fielded one of the best teams ever to play the game.

of ominous cracks in their morale, which is most important to be kept intact in a team that now has repeatedly tasted the pleasures of victory."[11] It had been more than a decade since a Philadelphia team had "tasted the pleasures of victory." Connie Mack's white elephants had been settling for peanuts since 1914. Now they wanted more.

The team opened the season on a hot pace, winning seven of the eleven games they played in April. Mickey Cochrane emerged as the on field general for the team, and his fiery competitiveness and hatred for losing symbolized the attitude of most of the A's players. Cochrane played like his hair was on fire, and when the Athletics lost a game, a teammate said, "You didn't want to get into the clubhouse with him. You'd be ducking stools and gloves and bats and whatever else would fly."[12] The only player on the team whose temper and hatred of losing eclipsed Cochrane's was Lefty Grove. Luckily, he hadn't been doing much of it lately. When relieved from a losing effort on the mound, Grove was known to tear off his uniform on the way to the clubhouse. Any loose objects were apt to become airborne, and water coolers were often the helpless objects of his tirades. Yes, Grove, Cochrane and the rest of the A's hated to lose. They would not have occasion to indulge that hatred very often in the 1929 season. In May, the Athletics won 22 of the 29 games played, and by the end of the month they already enjoyed a six-game lead over the St. Louis Browns and a seven-game lead over the Yankees. While the rest of the league waited for the A's to cool off, Connie Mack's boys kept winning games. The team went 24–9 in July, held its own in August, and by September 14, the Athletics had clinched the American League pennant.

By the end of the season, the A's had compiled a record of 104–46, best in franchise history, and 18 games in front of the second-place Yankees. Al Simmons once more led the team in offense, batting .365, belting 34 homers, and driving in a league-best 157 runs. Jimmie Foxx was close on his heels, posting the best year yet of his young career. Foxx hit .354 with 33 home runs and 118 RBIs. Cochrane and Bing Miller both batted .331, Jimmy Dykes hit .327, and Mule Haas had a breakout season, hitting .313 and swatting 16 home runs. With a team batting average of .295 and plenty of power, the A's had presented a formidable lineup for any starting pitcher. And their pitching wasn't bad either. George Earnshaw had

Two. Another Run at Greatness

rewarded Mack's confidence by leading the staff with 24 wins against eight losses. Lefty Grove finished the regular season with a record of 20–6, a 2.81 ERA, and for the fifth year in a row, led the American League in strikeouts, notching 170. In fact, Earnshaw's 149 strikeouts were second in the league and third among all major league pitchers. Rube Walberg threw in another 18 wins, while Ehmke, appearing in only 11 games, posted a record of 7–2. On both sides of the ball, the Athletics had power, experience, and consistency. They would be a hard team to beat in the World Series.

The 1929 Chicago Cubs felt they were more than a match for Connie Mack's boys. Their confidence was not unfounded. The Cubs were a powerhouse team in their own right. Led by their great second baseman, Rogers Hornsby, who led the team with his .380 batting average and 39 home runs, the Cubs fielded a deadly lineup of hitters. Outfielders Riggs Stephenson and Kiki Cuyler batted .362 and .360, respectively, and Hack Wilson hit .345 while tying Hornsby with 39 long balls. In fact, the Cubs boasted a team batting average of .303, eight points higher than the A's. The boys from Chicago were not slouches when it came to pitching, either. Though they had no standout aces like Lefty Grove or Earnshaw, they did have several good hurlers who were having very good years. Pat Malone led the Cubs with 22 victories, followed by Charlie Root with 19, Guy Bush with 18, and Sherriff Blake with 14. Malone was a fireballer who had notched 166 strikeouts during the season, best in the National League and placing him between Grove and Earnshaw as the top three strikeout artists in the majors. The Cubs were hungry for a championship. Like the Athletics, the Cubs had been in five previous World Series but they had only been victorious in one, and that was back in 1908. Chicago fans felt this was the time for their beloved Cubs to take the next step toward becoming a powerhouse team in their own right.

Babe Ruth, the face of the Murderer's Row Yankee team, went on record as believing that the A's were the better club and would win the series. He said he didn't anticipate

> any walk away, and the clubs are so closely matched that an upset is entirely possible. But whatever edge there is to one club or another goes, I think, to the Athletics. Taking all things into consideration I think they

have just a bit better balance, a bit better punch measured from top to bottom, and a bit more managerial experience. Connie Mack, wise to the ways of baseball and veteran of many a World Series contest, throws the balance in their direction. In a series in which pitching counts for much I think the A's are a bit better off for a few games than the Cubs. In addition to that they have the advantage of superior catching. I've been around baseball quite some time and I don't know of any catcher in the business who has more real receiving ability or who can get more out of pitchers than Mickey Cochrane.

Ty Cobb agreed with Ruth's assessment. "The Athletics will win the series because they have a superior pitching staff. The Cubs have no pitchers capable of stopping Foxx, Simmons and Miller. The Chicago batters don't like speed and they won't like Grove or Earnshaw."[13] Cobb, not one to easily dispense compliments, had been with the team for two years, and spoke with an insider's knowledge about their makeup and ability.

The series opened at Wrigley Field in Chicago on October 8, 1929. Mack shocked everyone in baseball when he announced that Harold Ehmke would take the hill to start Game One. Ehmke had seen only limited service during the regular season and had been informed by Mack that the team was not bringing him back at the end of the year. Ehmke did not resent Mack's decision. "I haven't helped you much this year, and it's lucky you didn't need me," he said. "But I've always wanted to pitch in a World Series, and I'd like to work in the series, if only for a few innings." Mack considered the request and came to the conclusion that Ehmke might be the perfect candidate to throw against the hard-hitting Cubs in the first game. After all, Ehmke's soft-throwing, submarine style might be just the thing to slow down Chicago's bats. Mack told Ehmke to take the last two series of the regular season off. "Go watch the Cubs in Philadelphia and New York. See what they like to hit, make notes on them, for I am going to pitch you in the first game."[14] In the meantime, the wily manager kept his decision a secret from the rest of the team and the baseball world.

Mack was as good as his word. Despite the fact that he had his aces, Grove and Earnshaw, available, Ehmke got the nod to face Charlie Root in the first World Series game ever to be played at Wrigley Field. Mack's decision proved to be pure genius. Ehmke kept the Cubs batters

Two. Another Run at Greatness

baffled all day. He scattered eight hits while striking out 13 Cubs with his slow, sidearm delivery, establishing a World Series record that would stand until 1953. Root was matching Ehmke pitch for pitch until the top of the seventh inning, when Jimmie Foxx launched a majestic home run to left-center field. Bing Miller drove in two insurance runs in the top of the ninth, and Ehmke held on for a 3–1 victory. While many sportswriters cringed when it was announced that Ehmke was the starter for Game One, they quickly reversed themselves at the game's conclusion to hail Mack as one of the best and smartest managers in the game.

Game Two was played the following day in Chicago. George Earnshaw was pitted against Pat Malone in the pitching matchup. Earnshaw's regular season performance had earned him this start, but there was more to it than that. Mack feared the powerful right-handed hitters in the Chicago lineup, particularly Rogers Hornsby, Hack Wilson, and Kiki Cuyler. Because of that, there would be no starts in this series for either Grove or Walberg. Grove was also having trouble with the tips of his fingers, and Cochrane stated that at times they bled when he pitched.[15] So Lefty, who was emerging as the ace of the staff, would be relegated largely to the role of reliever. He would not have to wait long to contribute in this capacity. Earnshaw was spotted to a three-run lead in the top of the third inning when Jimmie Foxx became the first player in baseball history to hit a home run in his first two World Series games. The A's added three more runs in the fourth, but Chicago mounted a threat in the bottom of the fifth. The Cubs got to Earnshaw for three runs and were threatening to get more when Connie Mack sent Grove to the mound to put out the fire. Grove closed out the inning without further damage, then went on to blank the Cubs in the final four frames. The A's added runs in their half of the seventh and eighth innings. The final result was a 9–3 victory for the boys from Philadelphia and the first save for Grove.

After a travel day, Game Three of the series was held at Shibe Park in Philadelphia on October 11, 1929. The Cubs sent Guy Bush to the mound to oppose George Earnshaw, who was pitching on short rest. Bush and Earnshaw dueled through the first four innings as neither team was able to score. The A's broke through with a run in the bottom of the fifth, but the Cubs answered quickly in the top of the sixth. Earnshaw started the sixth by walking his mound opponent. Chicago third baseman Norm McMillan then popped up a bunt attempt that was caught. Shortstop Woody English reached base on a costly error by Jimmy Dykes. Rogers Hornsby then singled to left field, plating Bush and tying the game. Hack Wilson hit a ground ball to second that should have gotten Earnshaw out of the inning, but it only accounted for the second out. Kiki Cuyler then singled to center, driving in both base runners and giving the Cubs a 3–1 lead. Bush allowed only one hit in his final four frames, and the Cubs made the 3–1 score stand up.

The next day the two teams met for one of the most exciting games in World Series history. Mack tapped Jack Quinn for the start against Charlie Root. The game started well for both pitchers, with neither team able to plate a run through the first three innings. In the top of the fourth, Charlie Grimm homered with Kiki Cuyler aboard, and the Cubs took a 2–0 lead. Things began to fall apart for the A's in the top of the sixth. Quinn gave up four straight singles to start the frame and the Cubs quickly added two more runs. Rube Walberg was brought in to relieve Quinn. Charlie Grimm laid down a bunt single that Walberg threw away in trying to make a play at first base. By the time the smoke cleared, two more runs had come in and Grimm was standing on third. Walberg got the next hitter out with a fly ball to center, but it was deep enough to bring Grimm home from third. Walberg struck out the next two batters, but the damage was done. The Cubs had a 7–0 lead, and Root was cruising. Eddie Rommel was brought in to pitch for the A's in the top of the seventh, giving the Cubs another run on a walk and two hits.

The Athletics went to the plate in the bottom of the seventh looking up from what seemed to be an insurmountable hole of 8–0. Al Simmons led off the inning with a home run. Foxx, Miller, Dykes, and Joe Boley all followed with singles, scoring two more runs. Mack then sent George Burns in to pinch-hit for Rommel, and Burns popped out to the shortstop. Max Bishop followed with a single that drove in Dykes, and Root was done for the day. Art Nehf took the ball and tried to close out the inning. Mule Haas was the first batter he faced, and

Two. Another Run at Greatness

Haas lifted a fly ball to center field that should have been an easy out. But Hack Wilson lost sight of it in the sun and the ball dropped in. By the time the ball was returned to the infield, Haas had cleared the bases with an inside-the-park home run, and the Cubs' lead had been cut to 8–7.

When Nehf walked Mickey Cochrane, Sheriff Blake was brought in to pitch to Al Simmons. Blake gave up back-to-back singles to Simmons and Foxx, scoring Cochrane and tying the game at eight. Pat Malone replaced Blake and became the fourth pitcher of the inning for the Cubs. He promptly hit Bing Miller with a pitch to load the bases for Jimmy Dykes. Dykes came through with a double that plated two more runs and gave the A's the lead for the first time in the game. Malone struck out Boley and Burns to end the inning, but the damage was done. The Athletics had accomplished the impossible, scoring 10 runs in the bottom of the seventh to pull ahead of the Cubs. It was, and remains, the greatest single game comeback in World Series history.

Lefty Grove came in to pitch for the A's in the top of the eighth. Grove slammed the door tightly on the Cubs' batters, facing the minimum six hitters in the final two frames and striking out four of them. The Cubs were crushed. They had been far out in front and should have evened the series, but the explosive offense of the A's had been too much for them to handle and they now found themselves behind three games to one in the series and on the verge of elimination.

October 13 was an off-day for the teams, with Game Five slated for Shibe Park on the 14th. President Herbert Hoover and his wife were in attendance, and everyone in the stadium felt that the Cubs would be the only ones making the long train ride back to Chicago. Mack surprised everyone by sending Ehmke to the mound for a second start in the series. The Cubs countered with Malone, and both pitchers worked scoreless frames through the third inning. In the top of the fourth, Ehmke got the first two outs before giving up a walk sandwiched between three hits. Rube Walberg was brought in to get the final out and hold the Cubs to a 2–0 lead. The two pitchers dueled through the final innings of the game, and when the Athletics came to bat in the bottom of the ninth, they were still trailing, 2–0. Malone struck out the first batter he faced before giving up a single to Max Bishop. Mule Haas followed with a home run to deep right field, and the game was tied. Malone then induced Cochrane to hit a ground ball to second, bringing Al Simmons to the plate. Simmons doubled, and Malone decided to intentionally walk the ever-dangerous Foxx, opting to take his chances with Bing Miller. But Miller came through with a two-out double that scored Simmons and secured the 3–2 victory for the A's and a 4–1 win of the series. Connie Mack and his white elephants had once more climbed to the top of the baseball world in winning their unprecedented fourth World Series title.

The 1930 baseball season opened with a dark cloud over the nation. Black Tuesday had shattered the stock market 15 days after the Athletics had won the World Series in 1929, plunging the country into the Great Depression. Philadelphians greeted the crisis with cheerful optimism at the beginning of 1930, but by the time the baseball season was slated to start, there were banks and businesses in the city closing their doors. The 1930 campaign was also the year Major League Baseball instituted some changes designed to increase the offensive portion of the game. A tighter wound ball and a more frequent substitution of new balls into a contest contributed to one of the most fantastic explosions of offensive firepower the game had ever seen. Nine of the 16 teams in the majors batted over .300, and the National League as a whole hit .303. Both leagues set record highs in home runs and runs scored, and the New York Yankees became the first team in history to score more than 1,000 runs in a season. All eight members of the St. Louis Cardinals' starting lineup finished the season with batting averages over .300, while Max Bishop's .252 average was not only the lowest among the A's starters, it was among the bottom five for all players with the qualifying number of at-bats in the majors. The 1930 season would prove to be a gold mine for hitters and a nightmare for pitchers, as ERAs skyrocketed. Ray Kremer was a 20-game winner for the Pittsburgh Pirates with an ERA of 5.02. Guy Bush, one of the Cubs' aces that had faced Philadelphia in the World Series, had the type of campaign in 1930 that could turn a pitcher's hair gray. He gave up a National League-record 155 runs on 291 hits for a whopping earned run average of 6.20. Despite that, he finished the season with a winning record of 15–10. The 1930 season was like that in baseball.

One pitcher who seemed totally unaffected by the changes was Lefty Grove. The 1930 slate would be one of Grove's best campaigns, as he finished with a record of 28–5, striking out a league-leading and career-best 209 batters. The most amazing stat for Grove was his 2.54 ERA, a full run lower than the next closest pitcher in the American League. In fact, the next lowest ERA on the Athletics belonged to Roy Mahaffey, at 4.19. Many of the A's batters benefited from the changes, none more than Al Simmons, who hit .381 to win his first American League batting crown. Mickey Cochrane slapped the ball around for an average of .357, while Jimmie Foxx hit .335 and belted a team-leading 37 home runs. In the 1930 campaign, the A's scored runs not only with their bats but with their legs as well. In a July 25 game against the Cleveland Indians the Athletics pulled off a triple steal not once, but twice, becoming the only team in major league history to execute a triple steal twice in the same game. By the time this season of the batter ended, Connie Mack's boys had complied a record of 102–52 to claim their ninth American League pennant, finishing eight games ahead of the Senators and 16 in front of the Yankees.

In the World Series, the A's faced the St. Louis Cardinals, who emerged victorious in a three-team race that went down to the final games of the season, finally edging out Chicago by two games. Though the Cardinals were led by Frankie Frisch, Chick Hafey, and Jim Bottomley, and every player on the team with more than 300 at-bats had an average over .300, Connie Mack's boys were still heavily favored to win their second consecutive Fall Classic, a feat that would give them two more championships than any other team in baseball.

In this year of the hitter, it would be the pitchers who emerged as the dominant force in the 1930 World Series. The lethal Cardinals' lineup would be held to a .200 average in the series, while the A's would bat only .197. Grove and Earnshaw had been held back the previous year in the series with Chicago, but they would now step forward to take control, pitching between them all but eight innings. The hard-throwing duo worked 44 innings, compiling an ERA of 1.02, striking out 29 and walking only 10. Though the Athletics had a horrible performance at the plate, 18 of their 35 hits went for extra bases, including six home runs, as the A's made their limited number of hits count more than the Redbirds.

Game One of the series was played in Philadelphia on October 1, 1930. Shibe Park was filled to overflowing with 32,295 fans expecting a high-scoring game. Lefty Grove took the mound for the Athletics, opposed by Burleigh Grimes, the spitballing ace of the Cardinals. Even though the spitball had been banned in baseball, a grandfather clause had been included so that existing spitball pitchers could continue to throw it for the duration of their careers. The A's struck first with a run in the bottom of the second inning. Jimmie Foxx connected for a one-out triple, and came home on a sacrifice fly by Bing Miller. In the top of the third, Grove uncharacteristically gave up three straight singles, and with the bases loaded, two sacrifice flies resulted in runs. The A's pulled even in the bottom of the fourth when Al Simmons launched a home run to the opposite field. The game remained tied into the bottom of the sixth, when Max Bishop's walk was followed by a run-scoring double by Jimmy Dykes. The A's added an insurance run in the bottom of the seventh, when Mule Haas tripled to right and came home on a sacrifice bunt by Joe Boley. Mickey Cochrane put the game away with a solo home run in the bottom of the eighth, and Grove shut the door to give Mack's boys a 5–2 victory. Graham McNamee, a renowned radio sports announcer of the era, reported the play-by-play during the series. After several innings of describing how Lefty's fastball was overpowering the St. Louis hitters, McNamee finally ran out of expletives and said simply, "Well, they can't hit 'em if they can't see 'em."[16]

Game Two the following day paired George Earnshaw against Flint Rhem. The A's took an early 2–0 lead in the bottom of the first inning, thanks to a home run by Mickey Cochrane and a run-scoring double by Jimmie Foxx. Spotted to this early advantage, Earnshaw never looked back. He gave up a run in the top of the second but then bore down to make short work of the Cardinal batters. Earnshaw pitched the full nine innings, striking out eight and allowing only one walk. The A's added a pair of runs in their half of the third and fourth innings to cruise to a 6–1 victory and a 2–0 lead in the series. Fans in Philadelphia were starting to predict a sweep.

Two. Another Run at Greatness

After a travel day, the series moved to Sportsman's Park in St. Louis for Game Three, on October 4. Nearly 37,000 Cardinal faithful crammed the bleachers to root for Bill Hallahan in his start against Rube Walberg. Hallahan gave up three singles in the top of the first but escaped the bases-loaded jam without giving up a run. The Athletics would not have another man reach third for the remainder of the game, as Hallahan scattered four more hits over the next eight innings. Taylor Douhit took Walberg deep in the bottom of the fourth inning to give the Cards a 1–0 lead, and that was all Hallahan needed. The Redbirds added another run in the fifth, two in the seventh, and a final tally in the eighth to walk away with a 5–0 win.

The Game Three victory convinced St. Louis fans that their team was back in the series and could win it all. On October 5, almost 40,000 spectators packed Sportsman's Park in hopes of seeing their Cardinals draw even with one more game at home. Game One winner Lefty Grove was back on the hill for the A's, opposed by future Hall of Fame knuckleballer Jesse Haines. The A's spotted Grove to a 1–0 lead in the top of the first when Max Bishop singled, advanced to second on a sacrifice, and took third on a wild pitch by Haines. Al Simmons then singled to bring Bishop home, ending the scoring drought that Philadelphia had suffered in St. Louis thus far. In the bottom of the third, Grove gave up a one-out triple to Charlie Gelbert, and Haines helped his own cause by rapping a single to bring Gelbert home. In the bottom of the fourth, Grove got Frankie Frisch to fly out to right field and struck out Jim Bottomley before Chick Hafey came to the plate. Hafey stroked a two-out double, and the Cards were in business again. Grove got the next batter, Ray Blades, to hit a ground ball to third. The inning should have been over, but Jimmy Dykes threw wildly to first base, allowing Blades to reach and Hafey to score. The next two Cardinals singled, driving in another run, before Grove got Haines to fly out to end the inning. Both of the runs were unearned, but St. Louis now held a 3–1 lead. Haines allowed no hits to the A's batters in the final five frames, allowing only three hitters to reach base on walks. Grove was the hard-luck loser of a 3–1 pitching duel in which both teams accounted for a total of only nine hits.

Game Five would prove to be an even better pitching duel than

Lefty Grove and the 1931 Philadelphia Athletics

Game Four, as George Earnshaw took the hill to face Burleigh Grimes. Through seven innings each pitcher had given up only two hits. Grove entered the game to relieve Earnshaw in the bottom of the eighth inning, even though he had pitched a complete game the previous day. Frankie Frisch managed a two-out single before Grove struck out Bottomley to end the frame. In the top of the ninth, Mickey Cochrane coaxed a walk from Grimes before Al Simmons popped out to short. Jimmie Foxx then stepped to the plate and belted Grimes' pitch over the wall in left to give the A's a 2–0 lead. Grove disposed of the Cards in the bottom of the inning to earn the win and a 3–2 Philadelphia lead in the series.

The series resumed at Shibe Park on October 8 with Earnshaw getting his third start against Bill Hallahan. The A's used two walks and two doubles in the bottom of the first to take a quick 2–0 lead. Hallahan had control problems in the second and gave way to Syl Johnson in the third. Jimmie Foxx greeted Johnson with a lead-off home run in the Athletic half of the third, and Jimmy Dykes swatted a two-run shot the following inning. Foxx then doubled in the fifth, advanced to third on a sacrifice, and scored on a Mule Haas flyout to give the A's a 6–0 lead. The Cardinals brought Jim Lindsey in to pitch the bottom of the sixth. Lindsey got Earnshaw to fly out to left, but then gave up a walk to Max Bishop. Jimmy Dykes doubled to left-center, and Bishop came in to score on a Michey Cochrane sacrifice fly. Earnshaw was brilliant, scattering three hits over the first eight innings to hold the hard-hitting Cards scoreless. In the top of the ninth, Earnshaw gave up a single and a walk before getting Frankie Frisch to line to first for what resulted in a double play. It looked as if he was going to post the shutout, but Chick Hafey rifled a double to left field to bring in a run before Earnshaw recorded the final out. The A's managed only seven hits but scored seven runs on the way to their best offensive outburst of the series, winning the game, 7–1, and clinching their second straight championship.

There was no doubt about it. The Yankees held sway over Major League Baseball from 1926–1928, winning two World Series titles in the process, but the Athletics were now at the top of the heap with a team every bit as fearsome as the Murderer's Row squads had been. With five world championships to their credit, they were not only the class of the American League, they were the greatest dynasty in Major League Base-

Two. Another Run at Greatness

ball to that point. Connie Mack's boys went into the offseason as the favorites to win their third straight pennant in 1931 and earn yet another trip to the Fall Classic. With their lineup of returning veteran stars, they also seemed a sucker's bet to become the first team in baseball history to win three straight World Series crowns.

Three
A Spring of Promise

When the Athletics reported to spring training at Terry Park Ballfield in Fort Myers, Florida, in the spring of 1931, everything pointed to another banner season for the white elephants from Philadelphia. The confines of Terry Park had been the spring destination of the Athletics since 1925, when Connie Mack had the stadium constructed as a spring training home for his team. Terry Park had served as a lucky charm of sorts for the team. That 1925 season had broken a losing streak of ten consecutive years, and had been the start of the team's resurgence that culminated in World Series victories in 1929 and 1930. Many of the star players currently on the team had never tasted a losing season in Philadelphia and had never started the season anywhere but Terry Park.

The players were confident about repeating as the American League champions. The New York Yankees and the Washington Senators would both field teams capable of contending for the title, but Connie Mack's boys liked their chances. Mack exuded an air of confidence that led him to uncharacteristically pick his boys during a pre-season interview. "We are starting off with the same team that won the October series last year," Mack stated to a reporter. "Whether the team will play up to that standard remains to be seen. There is nothing certain in this world, but I see no reason why the team as a whole should not play up to its form."[1]

Mack had good cause for his optimism. His team had ushered in the 1930s with one of the best performances in the history of the game. The A's could hit for average and power, and the comparisons had already been made between this lineup and the 1927 Murderer's Row of the New York Yankees. Jimmie Foxx, nicknamed "Double X" and the "Beast," was commonly referred to as the right-handed Babe Ruth. His towering blasts had become legend in the league, and Foxx didn't just hit home

THREE. *A Spring of Promise*

runs, he shattered the confidence of opposing pitchers. Yankees great Lefty Gomez, a Hall of Fame pitcher in his own right, paid tribute to Foxx's power many years later during the Apollo 11 landing on the moon. "When Neil Armstrong first set foot on the moon, he and all the space scientists were puzzled by an unidentifiable white object. I knew immediately what is was. That was a home run ball hit off me in 1933 by Jimmie Foxx." Gomez had come out on the losing end of many confrontations with Foxx over the years, prompting the Yankees' ace to make quips such as, "He could hit me at midnight with the lights out," and "He has muscles in his hair."[2]

Al Simmons naturally drew comparisons to the Yankees first baseman Lou Gehrig. Simmons was known as "Bucketfoot Al" for his tendency to step toward third base instead of toward the pitcher when swinging at the ball. This unorthodox style should have made him vulnerable at the plate, but it never became a hindrance, as he was one of the most feared sluggers in the game. Born Aloisius Szymanski, he had Americanized his Polish name while retaining a fierce pride in his Polish heritage. Thus far, in his seven-year career, he had never batted below .300, and in his last three seasons going into the 1931 campaign, he had batted .351, .365, and .381. But Simmons didn't just hit for average. Eighty-four of his 212 hits in 1929 had gone for extra bases, and he had improved on that number the following year, with 93 of his 211 hits going for more than a single. Foxx and Simmons were game-changers every time they stepped into the batter's box, and the A's one-two punch had all the explosive power of their Ruth-Gehrig rivals to the north.

One of the places the A's held an advantage over the Yankees was at the catcher's position. Mickey Cochrane had in a few short seasons established himself as the best catcher in the game. Not only did he call a great game and protect the plate like it was his own child, he was a natural-born leader and a great hitter in his own right. Cochrane had been one of the 1925 additions to the team that had started the Athletics on the road to being competitive in the league again. Cochrane oozed competitiveness, and his fiery spirit and desire to win became infectious among his teammates. He was the on-field general of the team, and this general hated to lose. He was prone to fits of temper when the A's blew a game, earning him the nickname of "Black Mike" in the clubhouse.

Al Simmons, the "Mr. Everything" of the Philadelphia A's. Simmons could hit for both average and power, and was an excellent outfielder. Known for his unusual style of "stepping into the bucket" when swinging at a pitch, Simmons was a beloved face of the franchise for most of his Hall of Fame career.

THREE. *A Spring of Promise*

But Cochrane was a real-life hero, on and off the field. On June 6, 1932, the Athletics were playing an exhibition in Cincinnati against the Reds. After the game the team traveled to Cleveland, where they took rooms in the Hollenden Hotel. Later that night, after many of the players had already gone to bed, word came that the Ellington Apartment Building, just across the street, was on fire. Jimmie Foxx looked out his window to see the complex engulfed in flames, and he could hear the screams of the inhabitants. One of the first people to go to the assistance of those trapped by the fire was Mickey Cochrane. With complete disregard for his own safety, Cochrane raced toward the burning inferno, followed by several members of the team. He helped police and firefighters rescue dozens of people from the flames amid frequent explosions and backdrafts. Cochrane single-handedly rescued three women and a man from a second-story window before returning to aide a 78-year-old man who was hanging from a fourth-story ledge. Along with Cy Peterman, a Philadelphia sportswriter, he held a fireman's net beneath the man while imploring him to jump. The man refused, stating that he had a Stratavarius violin in his hands, and he was afraid of breaking it. Though the wall the old man was clinging to seemed about to collapse, Cochrane refused to leave his post. At length, both man and violin were saved. Cochrane and several of the other players continued to aide in the rescue efforts until just before dawn. More than a dozen lives were lost in the fire, but dozens more were saved due to the selfless actions of Cochrane and his teammates. Truly, Mickey Cochrane was made of the right stuff to be the on-field general and leader of the team.[3]

The only member of the Athletics who hated losing more than Cochrane was Lefty Grove. Robert Moses Grove was born in the small western Maryland coal mining town of Lonaconing in 1900. Lefty did not finish school, completing only the first eight grades. He then followed his father and two older brothers into the mines. After only two weeks, however, Grove had made up his mind that he was not cut out to be a miner. He told his father that he didn't put the coal in the ground and didn't want to take any more of it out. Grove worked as a bobbin boy at a local silk factory and as an apprentice glass blower for a short period of time. When the glass factory burned down, Grove found summer employment laying track for the railroad. He worked at another glass factory as a needle etcher, earning the high salary of $5.25 per day at a time his father and brothers were averaging about $2 a day.[4]

Throughout this time, Grove had been playing baseball, or at least a version of the game. Most of the time the kids in the town had to play with homemade balls, and when bats were not available, they used slats from picket fences. Grove built his pitching arm by throwing rocks. By the age of seventeen, he began playing real baseball at First Field, the local baseball diamond. Games were held on Sundays, with the local boys taking on teams from nearby towns. Grove started out playing first base but was soon called on to pitch for the hometown squad. The games quickly became a favorite diversion for the residents of Lonaconing and were usually attended by a couple hundred spectators. Grove's pitching talent made him a hometown hero at an early age and gave him the opportunity to make money from his ability. In 1919, a local store owner sponsored a team from Lonaconing that played two games a week in a fenced park where they could charge spectators 25 cents admission to the games. At the end of the season, all players shared in the gate, which amounted to about $20 each. It was a small amount of money, but it was the first pay that Lefty ever received for playing baseball.[5]

Grove's hero was Walter "The Big Train" Johnson, the hard-throwing ace of the Washington Senators, and he made a few trips on the railroad between Cumberland, Maryland, and Washington, DC, to see his idol pitch in person. By 1919, Johnson had won more than 270 games in the big leagues. His career would conclude following the 1927 season with a record of 417–279, and Grove would get to pitch against boyhood hero for his final three seasons.

In 1919 Lefty emerged as a star in his own right when he pitched in a post-season game against the B&O Railroad team from Cumberland, Maryland. The Cumberland squad was one of the best teams in the area, and the manager made a practice of giving jobs to talented players as an inducement to play for him. Grove threw a no-hitter against the B&O boys, striking out 18 and allowing only one player to reach base in the entire game. The B&O manager was so impressed with Lefty's performance that he was heard to say he would give him a job with the

THREE. *A Spring of Promise*

railroad to make sure he pitched for Cumberland the next season. Sure enough, Grove landed a job as an apprentice mechanic for the railroad, but he would not play for the B&O team. A better offer was soon to come along.

In May of 1920 Lefty was given a contract to play for the Class C Martinsburg, West Virginia, team of the Blue Ridge League. He was to be paid a salary of $125 per month, more than twice the amount his father and brothers could make working in the mines. Grove played for Martinsburg for a short time, ending his stint there on June 25, 1920, when his contract was purchased by Jack Dunn, owner of the Double-A Baltimore Orioles of the International League. The Martinsburg team was short of money to complete the ballpark they played in, and though team management wished to keep Grove, he was traded to Baltimore for another player and the $3,000-$3,500 it would cost to build a fence at their home field. Lefty would later quip, "I was the only player ever traded for a fence."[6]

Grove joined the Orioles in the second half of the 1920 season and made his Baltimore debut on July 1. He gave up five hits while striking out four and walking three on the way to a 9–3 victory. He won his next two starts, throwing complete games, and Dunn was convinced that the $175 a month he was paying his new pitcher was a good investment. Dunn made the statement that he would not part with his budding ace for $10,000.

Grove would end the 1921 season with a record of 12–2. Over the next four years, he amassed a record of 96–34, winning 20 games in three different seasons and leading the International League in strikeouts every year. His 108 victories against 36 losses while pitching for the Orioles made him one of the biggest stars in the International League, and Dunn was constantly receiving offers from major league clubs wishing to obtain Grove's services. Dunn refused all offers, preferring to keep his young star in Baltimore, but by 1925 the Orioles were experiencing a shortage of cash, which prompted him to rethink Lefty's status. Following the conclusion of the 1924 season, Dunn approached Connie Mack to offer his star lefthander to the Athletics. Dunn demanded $100,600 for Grove's contract. The Orioles had sold the contract of another rising star several years before for $100,000, when Babe Ruth was dealt to the Boston Red Sox. Ruth's deal was the highest amount ever paid for a baseball player's contract until Lefty Grove came on the market. Mack, who was in the process of rebuilding his team in Philadelphia to make another run at the pennant, liked the idea of adding a strong, proven arm to his rotation and agreed to the asking price. Lefty Grove was to become one of the cornerstones around which Connie Mack would build his second dynasty in the American League, and his performance in Philadelphia over the next nine seasons would justify Mack's decision to spend the most money in the history of the game to add him to the A's staff.

Lefty had come a long way in five short years from the days when he had been traded for a fence. From 1925 through 1930, Grove won 115 games for the Athletics and recorded 20 or more victories his previous four seasons. He led the league in ERA and strikeouts several times, and along the way had earned a reputation as the best left-handed pitcher in the game and one of the best overall.

With Foxx, Simmons, Cochrane, and Grove as his nucleus, Connie Mack felt good about his chances to win a third consecutive pennant as the 1931 season was about to commence. A repeat as American League champions would mean that Mack's teams had won nine pennants. Boston and New York had each won six American League titles, and the Yankees were destined to put together a string of pennant-winning seasons that would see no equal in the history of the game. But for the moment, the Athletics stood as the class of the American League, if not baseball as a whole. The Yankees and the Washington Senators promised to present the biggest challenge to the Athletics winning their third straight pennant. New York had added to its already powerful lineup by signing future Hall of Fame infielder Joe Sewell during the offseason. The Senators had finished second in 1930, eight games behind the A's. The Yankees were a distant third, a full sixteen games off the pace. Yankees management hoped that the addition of Sewell would help them make up a few games in the standings and make them more competitive.

Connie Mack's only concern for the upcoming season was finding a third reliable starter to fit in the rotation with Grove and Earnshaw. Walberg was the natural choice, but his record in 1930 had been a dis-

THREE. *A Spring of Promise*

appointing 13–12, and he would have to improve on that mark if he hoped to hold onto his starting job. Regardless of his worries over his pitching staff, Mack was confident that his Athletics had enough arms to keep the team competitive and allow the offensive power and field defense to win games. In the meantime, he would keep his eyes open for any good hurler that might become available who could help the team. Mack told a sports reporter his goal for the A's was to win another pennant, and said the team had "proved it was a great ball club last season. It will be better this year.... I think we have an excellent chance of finishing on top again."[7]

Connie Mack had watched his team closely during spring training. Though this pre-season preparation was costly to the ownership of the team, Mack felt it to be money well spent. It not only put players "in good physical condition," it allowed managers "to size up their players and ascertain the potential strength of their teams." Mack also realized how sportswriters added to the bottom line of the team through the exposure they gave teams while in spring training. "Sports writers and photographers accompany the teams to each camp, so interest in baseball and the events of the approaching season are kept on the sports pages of our newspapers. This advance publicity is of inestimable value both to managers and to players."[8]

As the 1931 season was about to begin, the A's were getting more than their fair share of press exposure. Sportswriters believed that Mack's boys were destined to capture another world championship, and they scoured the fields and clubhouses for any new stories that would be of interest to baseball fans. Mack took full advantage of his team's celebrity status to add to the excitement of Philadelphia fans for the upcoming season, hoping to improve gate revenues, which had been sagging since the start of the Great Depression. The Athletics were the toast of baseball, but the hardships of the national economic dilemma were already starting to worry team management. With a roster filled with stars, the payroll for the A's was staggering. Two years of reduced attendance and gate revenue were causing ownership to worry about how long they could afford to keep the team together. As Connie Mack prepared his team for the trip north for Opening Day, he hoped that their performance on the field and a run for another title would lure more fans through the turnstiles at Shibe Park. If not, there would be some hard issues to be dealt with at the season's conclusion.

The Athletics opened the 1931 season on the road. Their first two series would be played against their greatest challengers to win the pennant: the Washington Senators and the New York Yankees. April 14 found the team at Griffith Stadium, in Washington, DC, where they were set to take on the Senators in a four-game series. Rube Walberg took the hill against Lloyd Brown in front of a large crowd that turned out to see if Walter Johnson's squad could start Connie Mack's boys out with a loss. Each team scored a run in their half of the first inning before the opposing hurlers settled in to a pitching duel. The score was still tied, 1–1, as the game moved into the bottom of the seventh, when Washington scratched out a run to take the lead. After a scoreless eighth, the A's were able to even the score with a tally in the top of the ninth that chased Brown from the game. Lefty Grove was brought in to pitch in the bottom of the frame. He blanked the Senators, sending the game to extra innings. When the A's scored a run in the top of the tenth, it looked as if the game was well in hand, but an unearned run by Washington in their half of the inning knotted things up again. The Senators sent General Crowder to the mound to begin the eleventh inning, and Philadelphia jumped on him for three hits and two runs before he could record the final out of the frame. Grove shut down the Senators in the bottom of the eleventh to earn his first win of the season and a 5–3 victory for Philadelphia. One game into the new campaign, the Athletics were showing the grit and resilience that had led them to consecutive titles and were playing like defending World Series champions.

April 15 found the team once more in Griffith Stadium for the second game of the series against the Senators. George Earnshaw faced Bump Hadley, Washington's 15-game winner from the previous year. The Senators took an early lead when they pushed across a run in the bottom of the third, and they chased Earnshaw in the bottom of the fourth when they erupted to put five more runs on the board. By the top of the sixth, the A's were trailing, 7–0. Philadelphia's bats were quiet, and the team was able to scratch out only four hits in the contest, scoring their solitary run in the top of the sixth. The team suffered its first loss of the year, 7–1, as both squads looked to the following day. On April

Three. *A Spring of Promise*

16, Connie Mack sent Hank McDonald to the hill to face General Crowder. Both teams brought their bats to the game this day, as neither starting pitcher was able to stay out of trouble or finish the game. Al Simmons rapped his first home run of the season, and the A's kicked in 10 more hits in a losing effort that saw Washington post a 5–4 victory.

April 17 was an off-day, and the teams resumed play on the 18th, with Mack sending his ace to the mound in hopes of earning a split in the series. Grove faced Sad Sam Jones as his pitching opponent. Jones was a competent hurler who had amassed a record of 15–7 the previous year, but all the smart money was still on Grove to earn his second victory of the season. Lefty struck out 10 batters and gave up only five hits in his eight innings of work, but the Senators scored two runs and led in the contest, 2–1. The A's had their chances. Washington pitching gave up eight hits, allowed two walks and hit Max Bishop with a pitch. Joe Cronin committed an error that allowed another Athletic to reach base safely, but eleven of the twelve Philadelphia base runners were stranded, as Jones worked in and out of trouble for more than six innings. Firpo Marberry took over in the sixth inning and closed the door, earning a save and a 2–1 victory for the team. Grove had come up short in a pitching duel in his first start of the young season, and the A's were limping out of Washington with a 1–3 record.

Things didn't get any easier for the white elephants when they arrived in New York for a game at Yankee Stadium on April 19. "The House that Ruth Built" was crammed to the rafters with more than 80,000 screaming fans who had turned out to see their 3–1 Yankees put Philadelphia in its place. In addition to the hostile crowd, the A's faced a potent New York lineup that featured six future Hall of Fame players: Earle Combs, Babe Ruth, Lou Gehrig, Tony Lazzeri, Bill Dickey, and Red Ruffing. Rube Walberg got the nod to face Red Ruffing, who had joined the Murderer's Row lineup the previous year in a mid-season trade with Boston. Walberg was spotted an early lead when the A's plated a run in the top of the first inning, and he made it stand up. The Yankees tied the game in the bottom of the sixth, but Philadelphia put up runs in the top of the seventh and eighth innings to take a 3–1 lead. New York scored in the bottom of the eighth but that was as close as they could come, as Walberg shut the door in the ninth, earning a 3–2 victory.

Lefty Grove and the 1931 Philadelphia Athletics

The following day, George Earnshaw took the mound against Hank Johnson. The A's jumped on Johnson early, scoring two in the first and two more in the third to take a 4-0 lead and chase the starter to the showers. Lefty Gomez came in to relieve Johnson and held the A's to only one hit in 3⅔ innings of work. In the meantime, the Yankees scored three runs of their own in the bottom of the fourth, powered by a two-run homer off the bat of Babe Ruth. The Sultan of Swat added another two-run dinger in the bottom of the eighth to give the Yankees the lead for the first time in the game, and Ed Wells pitched a scoreless ninth to hand the A's a 5-4 loss.

The two teams met at Yankee Stadium for the rubber game of the series on April 21. Roy Mahaffey got the start against Herb Pennock, the former Athletic who Connie Mack had traded away in 1915. Pennock was nearing the end of an illustrious career but was still considered to be an ace of the Yankees staff. He wouldn't have to be on top of his game this day, however, as his Yankee teammates scored early and often to give Pennock a comfortable lead. Mahaffey gave up two runs in the first and another two in the second before being chased in that frame without recording an out. Sol Carter replaced Mahaffey on the mound, but he could do little to stop the bleeding. Carter issued four walks to go along with five hits and gave up five more runs while retiring only one batter. Mack then turned to Eddie Rommel to try to get the A's out of the inning. Rommel posted the final two outs of the frame but not before giving up a run. At the end of two, the Yankees led the game, 10-0. New York added two more runs through the course of the game and took a 12-0 lead into the top of the ninth. The A's scored their only tally of the contest when Phil Todt drove in Mule Haas, and Pennock cruised to the 12-1 victory. After the first two series with their prime contenders for the pennant, the Athletics posted a dismal record of 2-5. The team prepared to travel to Philadelphia for their home opener against Washington, hoping to get hot and improve their record.

The Philadelphia fans were treated on April 22 by getting to see their ace take the mound in the home opener. Lefty Grove was slotted against Bump Hadley, and the matchup did not disappoint. The A's jumped on Hadley for four runs in the bottom of the first, chasing the starter after only one-third of an inning. Carl Fischer came in to relieve

Three. *A Spring of Promise*

Hadley and threw more than five innings of scoreless work to keep his team in the game, but the damage was already done. The only run the Senators scored came in the top of the second, when Joe Cronin took Lefty deep for a solo homer. Grove then bore down to shut the door on the Senators' batters for a 5–1 complete-game victory.

The A's took the next two games against the Senators to sweep the series and improve their record to 5–5. It wasn't quite the start Mack had in mind for his team, but it wasn't all that bad either, considering that one of the best players on the team was out of the lineup. Jimmie Foxx had not played since the second game in Washington. He had missed eight in a row, and the team had been without his offensive firepower. Foxx was back in the lineup on April 30, when the A's opened a short two-game homestand with the Yankees. But the powerful first baseman's return had little effect on the outcome of the game. Foxx went hitless in three official at-bats, reaching base one time on a walk. In the meantime, the A's had scratched out single runs off Yankees starter Hank Johnson in the first and third innings, and Rube Walberg carried the 2–0 lead into the top of the sixth. Walks, hits and an error plated three runs for the Yankees, who were still batting with only one out. Mack had seen enough. Walberg was pulled in favor of Hank McDonald, who put out the fire and closed the inning with no further damage. McDonald gave up another run in the top of the seventh, but the A's were still in the game. The Yankees blew the game open in the top of the ninth, tacking on three insurance runs, and went on to record the 7–2 victory.

George Earnshaw started the month of May with a win, shutting down the powerful Yankees lineup with a three-hit shutout in a complete-game performance. Philadelphia stroked nine hits, including home runs by Mickey Cochrane and Mule Haas that accounted for four runs. The A's had once more pulled even with a 6–6 record, but they found themselves in sixth place in the American League, ahead of only the Boston Red Sox and St. Louis Browns. Rube Walberg put the team on the winning side of the ledger with a masterful performance and a complete-game victory at Washington, scattering seven hits to earn a 3–1 victory on May 3.

On May 4, the A's opened a three-game series with the Boston Red Sox at Shibe Park. The White Elephants suffered a hard loss, giving up

15 hits in a 7–5 defeat. Almost a week into the second month of the season found the team with a disappointing .500 record and not performing like defending World Series champions. But this was to be the last loss the Athletics would suffer in quite some time. The month of May would belong to the A's, as the team started a tear that would become one of the longest winning streaks in major league history. By the time this winning streak ended, Philadelphia would rise to the top of the league standings and never look back.

Four
Seventeen Games in a Row

Through the first week in May, Connie Mack had reason for concern over the way his club was playing. In Florida, he worried about finding a third reliable starter to join Grove and Earnshaw in the rotation, but he had been confident about the team's ability to hit the ball. Fourteen games into the season found several A's struggling at the plate, however, including the mighty Jimmie Foxx. Bing Miller was hitting only .184, Joe Boley a weak .125, and Jimmie Foxx had a minuscule average of .095. Mickey Cochrane and Al Simmons were having early success at the plate, and both were flirting with .350 averages. Mule Haas was swatting a respectable .283, as was Doc Cramer at .273, but more production was needed from the middle of the lineup. Mack was sure that Miller, Boley and Foxx would break out of their slumps, but he could have had no idea that an offensive explosion was about to take place. Over the next three weeks, Boley would raise his average 63 points, Miller would climb to a respectable .281, and Foxx would go on a rampage, raising his average to .283 while swatting seven home runs. Cochrane and Simmons continued to set the pace, and by the end of this stretch they would both be hitting over .400 for the season.

The streak began on May 5 at Shibe Park when the A's faced the Boston Red Sox in the second game of the series. George Earnshaw took the mound against Ed Durham in what was a pitchers' duel for most of the game. Philadelphia took an early 1–0 lead in the bottom of the first inning before both hurlers settled in to post zeros on the scoreboard through six innings. In the top of the seventh, Earl Webb hit a home run off Earnshaw to tie the game, but the A's answered with a tally of their own in the bottom of the frame to go on top again. Two insurance runs in the bottom of the eighth put the game away, and Earnshaw earned the complete-game victory to even his record at 2–2. The rubber game of the series pitted Eddie Rommel against Boston's Jack Russell. This game was anything but a pitchers' duel, as both teams smacked the ball around the park. Rommel went the distance, even though he allowed 11 hits against the Boston batters. But the knuckleballer only gave up three runs, largely because he did not issue any free passes. The A's recorded 18 hits to go along with three walks. Cochrane and Foxx each hit home runs, the first of the season for Foxx, and Philadelphia cruised to a 10–3 win.

May 9 found the A's at Sportsman's Park in St. Louis to start a series against the Browns. Rube Walberg took the mound against Sam Gray. Walberg got into trouble in the bottom of the first when the Browns took a 1–0 lead. He gave up single tallies in the third, fifth and seventh, and going into the top of the eighth, the Athletics were trailing in the game, 4–1. In the top of that frame, Philadelphia took advantage of a St. Louis error to put five unearned runs on the board, powered by a three-run homer by Jimmie Foxx, his second long ball in two days. Lefty Grove was brought in to replace Walberg in the bottom of the eighth, and he struck out four of the six men he faced to secure the win and earn his first save of the season.

After two days off, Connie Mack sent Lefty Grove to start the game on May 12 against Pat Caraway and the Chicago White Sox at Comiskey Park. Philadelphia scored in its half of the first three innings, and Grove was staked to a 4–0 lead. That was all he would need. Lefty allowed the White Sox only four hits while surrendering one earned run in a complete game 4–2 victory. The team had won four in a row, and had moved into first place in the American League standings.

George Earnshaw started the second game of the series against Tommy Thomas in what could best be described as a marathon. The White Sox held a 5–3 lead through seven innings before the A's staged a late-game comeback with runs in the eighth and ninth innings to tie the score. They made the most of a Chicago error, scoring two unearned tallies. Earnshaw and Thomas both pitched scoreless frames in the tenth, and Red Faber was brought in to pitch the top of the eleventh for Chicago. Faber was touched for two runs, and Earnshaw made them stand up, shutting the door in the bottom of the inning to secure the 7–

Four. Seventeen Games in a Row

5 victory. Philadelphia went for a sweep of the series on May 14, when Rube Walberg took the hill to face Chicago's Vic Frazier. The A's chased Frazier after five innings, scoring four runs. Ted Lyons was brought in to relieve the starter, and he allow one more run in four innings of work. In the meantime, Walberg scattered seven hits, allowing only two runs in his nine innings of work. The 5–2 win was Philadelphia's sixth in a row, and Walberg, the pitcher Connie Mack had been worried about during the preseason, was now leading the staff with a 5–1 record and a 2.40 ERA.

The A's continued their road trip on May 15, when the team arrived in Cleveland to take on the Indians at League Park. Eddie Rommel took the ball for Philadelphia, opposed by Clint Brown for the Tribe. Neither pitcher surrendered a run through six innings of work, but the A's broke through in the top of the seventh for a 1–0 lead. Two more runs were plated in the eighth and one in the ninth to give Rommel a 4–0 lead. Eddie had all the run support he would need after the seventh, however, as he scattered nine hits in a complete-game shutout. Lefty Grove faced Willis Hudlin the following day in what should have been an easy victory for the Athletics. But Grove was not his usual, overpowering self. The big lefthander was touched for twelve hits in nine innings of work, surrendering five runs. Pitching was not the order of the day, however, as Grove was the beneficiary of twenty Philadelphia hits, and an offensive display that saw the A's score nine runs in their last two at-bats. The final result was a 12–5 victory for the white elephants and their eighth win in a row.

The third game of the series, played on May 17, proved to be a repeat of the slugfest from the previous day. George Earnshaw opposed Wes Ferrell in a game where neither starter was able to get the other team out. Each starter gave up two home runs. Earnshaw surrendered nine runs through 4⅓ innings, while Ferrell gave up ten through 5⅓. Hank McDonald replaced Earnshaw and stopped the bleeding, allowing the Indians only one run in four innings of work. Two different Indian relievers gave up a total of five runs to the A's in the final two frames, and Lefty Grove came in to close out the contest and earn his second save of the year in the 15–10 win. The final game of the series pitted Rube Walberg against Jake Miller. The Philadelphia bats had awakened at just the right time to cover for the pitching that had gone south. Walberg was pounded for seven runs on twelve hits and seven walks through 7⅓ innings, but the A's rapped out thirteen hits of their own, resulting in ten runs on the scoreboard. Lefty Grove pitched a scoreless 1⅔ innings to give Walberg the win and earn his third save.

Philadelphia had won all four games played in Cleveland, but the pitching staff must have been glad about leaving the Indians behind as the team traveled to Detroit to open a three-game series with the Tigers. The change of scenery at Navin Field would prove to have a good effect on the A's hurlers. Earnshaw toed the rubber against the veteran Waite Hoyt on May 19 and turned in a stellar performance. He allowed only two hits while blanking the Tigers for nine innings. Philadelphia drove in five runs on nine hits for the 5–0 win. The victory allowed the A's to maintain a two-game lead over Ruth, Gehrig, and the rest of the Yankees, who were trying hard to keep pace.

On May 20, Lefty Grove took the hill against George Uhle. Grove was having a good season thus far with a record of 4–1 and had notched a few saves, but he was not the leading pitcher even on his own team. Rube Walberg, the pitcher Mack had been worried about in his starting rotation, had emerged as the ace of the A's through this part of the season and was sporting a record of 6–1. Grove needed a couple victories to catch up to Walberg, and his matchup against Uhle promised to be a step in that direction. Known for his intense competitive drive and fiery temper, Grove was all but unapproachable on days that he was scheduled to pitch. Teammates and sportswriters knew to walk a wide path around the hot-headed hurler. Jimmy Dykes said that "on the day he was pitching it was suicide for a photographer to take his picture. He'd throw the ball right through the lens." Mickey Cochrane knew how to harness Grove's temper for the good of the team. Whenever he would notice that some of the zip was missing from Lefty's fastballs, he would call time, go to the mound, and ask Grove if he needed to be relieved. Cochrane said that Grove always got the look of "an insulted artist." He would unceremoniously tell the catcher to get back behind the plate where he belonged and leave the pitching to him. Cochrane said, "I went back and he nearly tore my hand off with fireballs that the hitter hadn't seen. Lefty had been unconsciously letting up, and when

Four. Seventeen Games in a Row

he got sore at me he wanted to knock me out of the park with every pitch." Cochrane would also shout insults at Grove when he thought the pitcher wasn't performing to his capacity. The result was always the same, an outpouring of unhittable fastballs. Grove later admitted that he was sometimes madder at Cochrane than he was at the opposing hitters.[1] When Grove took the mound against Uhle and the Tigers' hitters, he was in top form. He allowed only three hits while going the distance for a complete-game victory. Jimmie Foxx and Bing Miller each hit homes runs, accounting for more run support than Lefty would need to earn the 3–0 victory.

Eddie Rommel got the start on May 21 against Tommy Bridges. Rommel lasted just over an inning but had a 2–1 lead when he handed the ball over to Roy Mahaffey. Both teams brought hot bats to the contest, as they combined for 32 hits and 17 runs. But the power of the A's proved to be the difference. Philadelphia clubbed three home runs, Mickey Cochrane had four RBIs, Eric McNair and Bing Miller each drove in three, and the Athletics emerged victorious, 12–5.

After an off-day, the A's returned to Philadelphia for a short one-game series with the Boston Red Sox on May 23. George Earnshaw faced Boston's Ed Durham in front of a small crowd of about 10,000 fans at Shibe Park. Though the team was now in first place and had won fourteen in a row, the effects of the Great Depression were being felt in Philadelphia, as many people simply did not have the extra money to take in a ball game. Those that did have the price of a ticket that day were treated to a gem. The A's jumped on Durham for four runs in the bottom of the first inning, chasing the starter before he could record the second out of the frame. They added two more in the second, and Earnshaw was on his way. George scattered four Boston hits and struck out six on his way to a 7–1 complete-game victory.

May 24 found the team at Yankee Stadium for a one-game set with New York. Connie Mack must have been envious as he eyed the crowd of 45,000 gathered to watch his team take on their beloved Yankees. It was more than four times the number of fans that had showed up in Philadelphia to watch their front-running team in the last home game. Rube Walberg opposed Red Ruffing in a game that gave the hometown New York fans little to cheer about. The A's scored a run in the top of

Jimmie "The Beast" Foxx. Heralded as the right-handed Babe Ruth, Foxx hit for average power as one of the most feared long-ball threats in baseball. At the time of his retirement, Foxx was second only to Babe Ruth in career home runs.

Four. Seventeen Games in a Row

the second inning to jump into the lead, then tacked on three more in the top of the fourth. That was all Walberg would need. Rube was in trouble several times during the course of the game, allowing eleven hits and six walks, but he was able to induce two double plays and stranded eleven Yankee runners to escape with only three runs surrendered and a 7–3 win. Jimmie Foxx belted a home run, his sixth of the season, as he went 2-for-4 and lifted his batting average to .274.

Foxx's hot bat had helped to drive the A's current winning streak, as the popular first baseman showed flashes of the power that made him one of the most feared hitters in the American League. At the plate, Foxx lived up to one of his popular nicknames: "The Beast." For twelve consecutive seasons he hit 30 or more home runs, and he drove in 100 or more for thirteen straight years. But once he was out of the batter's box, Jimmie Foxx was anything but "The Beast." He loved his fellow man as much as he loved baseball, and his heart was as mighty and full as his home run swing. Foxx always made time to accommodate fans, especially children, and he frequently spoke to school-age kids about the importance of staying in school and finishing their education, despite or possibly because of the fact that he had quit to play baseball. He used his salary from the A's to financially support his parents and his brother, even though he had lost all of the money he had previously saved in the stock market crash of 1929. Known as a great tipper around Philadelphia, he was also a noted check snatcher, and would usually pick up the tab for any dinner or outing he attended. One story of his generosity involved an opposing player from the Chicago White Sox. Billy Sullivan Jr. had just been called up to the big team from Notre Dame and was penciled in to play first for Chicago. He had finished infield practice before the game, and had thrown down his glove before taking his place in the dugout. Foxx picked up the glove, examined it, and yelled to Sullivan, "We don't use gloves like this up here. It's too small." Sullivan told him it was the only one he could find in South Bend before leaving for Chicago. The next day, Foxx came out of the dugout holding two gloves in his hands. He handed one of them to Sullivan, saying, "Take it, it's yours." It was a perfectly broken in first baseman's mitt, Foxx's gift of encouragement to a rookie from the opposing dugout.[2]

Lefty Grove and the 1931 Philadelphia Athletics

May 25 opened a five-game series in Philadelphia between the Yankees and the A's with a doubleheader. New York was 5½ games behind the front-running Athletics, and if they were going to make up ground, now was the time to do it. Connie Mack must have been thrilled by the 35,000-plus fans who crammed Shibe Park to attend the opener, and he probably smiled to himself over the fact that more than three times the number of people who had attended the last home game had come to see his boys battle the famed Murderer's Row lineup, including Ruth, Gehrig, Combs and Dickey. Mack sent his ace to the mound in this game, as Lefty Grove faced Hank Johnson. The Yankees jumped out to a 2–0 lead in the top of the second, the big blow being a home run from right fielder Ben Chapman. Grove then bore down to keep New York scoreless for the remainder of the game, holding Ruth, Gehrig and Dickey hitless for the day. In the meantime, Philadelphia rallied for three runs in the bottom of the third and tacked on an insurance tally in the eighth for the 4–2 win. Grove was now 6–1 with an incredibly low 2.05 ERA.

In the second game of the twinbill, Philadelphia made a statement, not just to the Yankees, but to the entire American League. In a 16–4 pounding of New York, the A's proclaimed that they were the current class of the league, as they won their seventeenth straight game. Roy Mahaffey was the benefactor of this offensive outpouring that saw 25 A's runners reach base. Philadelphia now boasted a record of 24–7 and enjoyed a five-game lead over second-place Washington. The slow start that had resulted in a 7–7 record after the first couple weeks of the season was now forgotten, and the team seemed unstoppable. Indeed, a casual glance at the A's starting lineup must have been intimidating to any team hoping to oust them from the top spot in the standings. Foxx had gotten his home run swing back, had raised his average to .284, and he was at the bottom of the list, so far as the Philadelphia stars were concerned. Mule Haas was hitting .315, which paled in comparison beside the .393 average Mickey Cochrane was boasting. Top honors, however, belonged to Al Simmons, whose torrid pace at the plate had led to an unbelievable .426 average. With arguably the best pitching staff in the league, and with all of their star batters now hitting up to their potential, it seemed as if the A's were a team of men playing in a league with boys, and one

FOUR. *Seventeen Games in a Row*

could only wonder when they would finally lose a game. That loss was soon to come, but the team decided not to make a habit of it. In fact, they would lose only 38 more times over the course of the season, and ten of these would come in the month of September, after they had the pennant wrapped up and were looking ahead to their third consecutive trip to the World Series.

Five
The Boys of Summer

All good things must come to an end, and for the Athletics the seventeen-game winning streak came to a close on May 26 against their hated rivals, the Yankees. New York sent its ace, Lefty Gomez, to the hill to start the third game of the series. Mack gave Eddie Rommel the nod to oppose him. It was a rough day for Rommel and his knuckleball, and he was back in the clubhouse after only two innings of work. Babe Ruth hit a solo home run and Bill Dickey drove in three in a 10-hit attack that resulted in six runs for the Yanks. Gomez scattered seven hits in a complete-game performance that earned a 6–2 victory for New York and ended the A's winning ways at seventeen consecutive games. With less than a week remaining in the month, it was only the second loss for Philadelphia in May.

One streak had ended, but another was to begin shortly. Lefty Grove was soon to begin a consecutive win streak that would challenge the existing American League record. It would be a personal streak, but as Grove went, so went the A's, and the big, lanky lefthander spent most of the summer months piling up victories that helped the team hold off their challengers and remain in first place. Lefty was about to have his best season in professional baseball, and by the end of the year he would be acclaimed as the best player in the American League.

On May 27, George Earnshaw took his 5–2 record to the mound to face George Pipgras of the Yankees in the fourth consecutive game against their hated rivals. Neither pitcher had a particularly good outing, as the batters combined for 23 hits and five walks. The Yankees out hit the A's, 12–11, but Earnshaw was able to emerge victorious in a 6–5 win that saw Philadelphia score two runs in the bottom of the ninth inning to come from behind. The following day was the conclusion of the five-

FIVE. *The Boys of Summer*

game series, and Rube Walberg was set to go against Red Ruffing. The teams would have a comparable number of base runners to the previous day, as 22 reached by base hits and six through walks and errors. The Yankees compiled a 4–0 lead through the top of the sixth inning, as everything looked to be going their way. Philadelphia managed a single run in the bottom of the sixth, and Earnshaw pitched a scoreless frame in the New York half of the seventh. The A's then tied the contest with three runs in the bottom of the frame, and Lefty Grove was brought in to relieve Earnshaw when the team took the field. Grove pitched two innings of scoreless ball, and the A's rallied for a run in the bottom of the ninth to seal the win and boost Lefty's record to 7–1. They had also taken four of five from the Yankees and made a statement of dominance in the league.

After a day off on May 29, the A's traveled to Boston to open a series of back-to-back doubleheaders with the struggling Red Sox. Even though Grove had pitched against the Yankees two days before, he was given the start against Boston's Jack Russell. Grove gave up several hits and allowed an unusual number of walks but was able to make pitches when he needed to and kept the Red Sox off the scoreboard through nine innings of work. But Russell was up the challenge, and after regulation, the teams were locked in a 0–0 tie. Grove and Russell blanked the opposing hitters in the tenth and eleventh innings, and the game moved into the twelfth still knotted up. The A's exploded for five runs in the top of the twelfth, and Grove even contributed an RBI hit. Lefty closed the door in the bottom of the frame, taking the first meeting of the series, 5–0, and raising Grove's record to 8–1.

Roy Mahaffey faced Ed Durham at Fenway Park for the second game of the double feature. The A's took an early 2–0 lead in the top of the second, added two more in the top of the fourth, and an insurance tally in the fifth. Mahaffey held the Red Sox scoreless through eight innings, and it looked like the Athletics were cruising to an easy victory. But the wheels came off the cart in the bottom of the ninth. Mahaffey seemed to tire and ran into trouble with the Boston hitters. By the time Connie Mack pulled him from the game he had recorded only one out in the inning, and the Red Sox were threatening to tie the contest. Eddie Rommel was brought in to stop the bleeding, but he gave up a hit and a walk without retiring a single Boston batter. Mack then turned to Rube Walberg. But this was to be Boston's day. Walberg surrendered a walk and a hit. Two runs charged to Rommel crossed the plate, and the Red Sox escaped with a 6–5 victory. Bob Kline, who had come in to relieve Durham in the top of the eighth, got the win and Rommel took a hard-luck loss.

On May 31, the A's closed out their four-game series with Boston by playing another doubleheader. George Earnshaw faced Milt Gaston in game one, and the Red Sox jumped out to an early lead when they scored two runs in the bottom of the first. Philadelphia rallied, scoring three in the top of the third and chasing Gaston to an early shower. Hod Lisenbee took over for Gaston, but he had no more success getting out the Athletics' batters than the starter had. Lisenbee gave up three more runs in the top of the fourth and another in the fifth. Earnshaw gave up ten hits but managed to strand six of the runners to record his seventh victory in a 7–4 win. In the nightcap, Hank McDonald took the mound against Ed Morris. The Red Sox scored a run in the bottom of the third, but the A's tied it in the top of the fourth. Boston added another run in their half of the frame, but Philadelphia scored two in the top of the fifth to take its first lead in the contest. It was short-lived. Boston scored two in the bottom of the fifth and added three more in the sixth to coast to a 7–3 win. Connie Mack's boys had definitely cooled off. After taking four of five from the mighty Yankees, they had been able to do no better than earn a split with the cellar-dwelling Red Sox.

June 1 was a travel day, and the second found the A's back in the friendly confines of Shibe Park, ready to open a series with the Chicago White Sox. Rube Walberg got the start against Pat Caraway, and he pitched a gem. After giving up two runs in the top of the first inning, Walberg settled down to put zeros on the board for the next eight innings. In the meantime, the A's cut the deficit in half with a run in the bottom of the first, and Bing Miller's two-run homer in the bottom of the sixth provided the margin for a 3–2 victory. Walberg's record was now 8–1. The pitcher Connie Mack had worried about at the beginning of the season and who had been in danger of losing his spot in the starting rotation now had the same record as Lefty Grove. But that would not last long.

FIVE. *The Boys of Summer*

On June 3, Grove took the mound against Chicago's Ted Lyons. Lyons' record was 2–0, and he had a respectable 3.00 ERA, so the game promised to be a pitchers' duel. It did not disappoint. Grove and Lyons battled through nine innings, almost matching one another pitch for pitch. The A's scored an early run in the bottom of the second to take a 1–0 lead, but Chicago tied it up with a run of their own in the fifth. Philadelphia got another run in the seventh, and Lefty made it stand up, pitching scoreless ball in the eighth and ninth to earn the 2–1 victory and improve his record to 9–1.

On June 4, George Earnshaw faced the struggling Tommy Thomas. The A's got to Thomas in the second for two runs to take the lead. Earnshaw, who allowed only three hits in the game, gave up a run in the top of the third to make the contest interesting. But the A's tacked on single tallies in the fifth and seventh to open up a 4–1 lead, and Earnshaw bore down to blank the White Sox the rest of the way. The series finale was played on June 5, and featured Roy Mahaffey against Chicago ace Red Faber. The A's got to Faber early, however, scoring four runs in the first two innings and chasing the starter after only 1⅔ innings of work. With a 4–1 lead, it looked as if Mahaffey was going to have an easy day. But Garland Braxton held Philadelphia for the next 3⅓ innings, surrendering just one unearned run, as he kept the game from getting away and gave his team a chance to win. In the meantime, the White Sox scored two more runs and the game was 5–3 at the end of five. Mahaffey gave up another run in the top of the sixth, and was lifted with two outs for Hank McDonald, who retired the final Chicago batter to end the frame. Lefty Grove was brought in to pitch the top of the seventh, and he uncharacteristically gave up a run to tie the game. White Sox manager Donie Bush had brought Hal McKain in to pitch in the bottom of the sixth, and the move proved to be a stroke of genius. McKain baffled the A's hitters, putting on a masterful display of pitching, and by the end of nine innings the game was still tied. Grove and McKain continued to duel through the tenth and eleventh, with neither hurler allowing a run. In the top of the twelfth, Grove was touched for two runs. McKain held Philadelphia scoreless in the bottom of the frame, and the White Sox claimed the 7–5 win. It was a hard loss for Grove. He ended up throwing six innings on short rest after having gone the distance in a pitchers' duel two days before. The seven hits and one walk he surrendered in his six innings of work in this game would seem to show that he had little left in the tank after fifteen innings in the afternoon June sun.

By today's standards, Mack's usage of Lefty would be unthinkable, but during this era pitchers were not specialists, they were expected to earn their keep. Connie Mack expected his ace to not only be a winner, but to be a workhorse as well, burning up a large amount of innings for the team. For his part, Grove did not mind the work. In fact, he relished it. What he couldn't abide, however, was losing. After the game on June 5, Lefty threw one of his patented tirades in the locker room. Jimmy Dykes said, "He was so mad he didn't talk to anyone. He got into his Pierce Arrow and drove to his home in Lonaconing, Maryland. He didn't show up at the park for three days."[1] Mack was used to such tantrums from his star pitcher, and usually handled them with calm diplomacy. He never used Grove's nickname, always addressing him as Robert, and his tone of voice never gave the slightest intimation that he was upset or irritated by Lefty's erratic behavior. While most of Lefty's teammates seemed cowed by his high-strung antics, Mack remained unimpressed. Once, when he had gone to the mound to take Lefty out of a game, he held out his hand for the ball, to which Grove snapped, "Go take a shit." Keeping his hand outstretched and looking Lefty right in the eye, Mack responded calmly, "You go take a shit, Robert."[2] When Grove returned to Philadelphia in time for his next scheduled start, on June 8, Mack greeted him in a casual manner and simply inquired if the temperamental star was ready to get back to work. Grove was ready. June 5 had been the end of an eight-game winning streak for him, but he was about to embark on another undefeated stint that would dwarf that effort and put him in line to set the American League record for consecutive victories by a pitcher. The current record was sixteen games, set in 1912 by both Smoky Joe Wood and Walter Johnson.[3] Grove would not suffer another loss for more than two months, as he closed on the record jointly held by his boyhood hero. The team had already won seventeen in a row. Now Lefty would try to achieve that same streak of consecutive victories on a personal level.

While Grove was back in Lonaconing, the team opened a series with the Detroit Tigers. Rube Walberg took on Waite Hoyt in front of a

Five. The Boys of Summer

Saturday afternoon crowd of only 15,000 fans. Mack must have been worried over the attendance at Shibe Park. They had packed the place when the Yankees came to town, but fans didn't seem to care as much about seeing the other teams in the league play. The Tigers got to Walberg for a run in the first, but the A's pulled even in the bottom of the fourth. Detroit got that run back in the top of the fifth and took a 2–1 lead. Philadelphia went wild on the bases in its half of the inning, and by the time the dust had settled on the field they had scored seven runs to take a commanding 8–2 lead. Each team had a three-run inning in the final frames, and the Athletics cruised to an 11–5 victory. Walberg improved to 9–1, a better record than Lefty Grove.

On Sunday, June 7, the A's scored early and often in a fifteen-hit attack that plated twelve runs. Jimmie Foxx and Bing Miller each hit home runs and drove in four on the way to the 12–2 rout that gave Roy Mahaffey the win and dropped the hapless Vic Sorrell to a 2–6 record. Grove returned to pitch the third game of the four-game series, and was opposed by Earl Whitehill. Lefty mixed in seven hits with eight strikeouts and held the Tigers scoreless for seven innings after giving up two runs in the top of the first. In the meantime, the A's went to work, fueled by a two-homer, four-RBI performance by Jimmie Foxx, and by the end of eight full held a 7–2 lead. Grove gave up a meaningless run in the top of the ninth before getting the third out for the 7–3 win. It was his tenth victory of the young season, and the first in what was soon to become a memorable streak.

The final game of the set paired George Earnshaw against Tommy Bridges. Each team scored two runs in the third inning before the game settled into a pitching duel for the next three frames. Detroit scratched out a run in the top of the seventh to take a short-lived 3–2 lead. The A's responded in their half of the inning by putting up five runs, and repeated the act in the bottom of the eighth to take a 12–3 lead. The scoring deluge was accomplished mainly with singles and doubles. There was only one home run hit by Philadelphia, and it was not struck by Foxx, Simmons, Cochrane, or even Haas. George Earnshaw went deep to help his own cause on a day when he was the hottest hitter on the A's team, going four-for-five and driving in two runs. Earnshaw improved to 9–2, as he, Walberg and Grove vied to see who would emerge as this

Lefty Grove and the 1931 Philadelphia Athletics

year's ace in Philadelphia. One thing was already established: the Athletics had the most dominant pitching rotation in the American League. Forty-six games into the season saw their top three pitchers combining for just under thirty wins as the most potent one-two-three rotation in the game.

After a day off, the A's opened a four-game series with the St. Louis Browns at Shibe Park on June 11. The Browns were near the bottom of the league, and with the way Philadelphia was playing, Athletics fans were expecting a sweep. Wally Hebert got the start for St. Louis. It was his first game in the majors, and he faced the league's top team in front of a very hostile stadium of spectators. Above that, Hebert was matched up against Rube Walberg, the veteran ace whose 9–1 record was among the best in the league. Everything pointed to an easy win in game one, but no one bothered to let Hebert know how hopeless his situation was. The twenty-three-year-old rookie took the mound to pitch the game of his life that Thursday afternoon. In a complete-game effort that saw him scatter seven hits and five walks, he allowed only one earned run. The Browns got to Walberg early in the top of the first by plating three runs, then added three more in the top of the seventh and two in the eighth on a fourteen-hit attack that featured home runs by Goose Goslin and Jack Burns. Walberg looked like the rookie, and Hebert pitched like an ace in a game where role reversal seemed to be the order of the day. Hebert would only spend four years in the majors, all of which would end in losing records with high ERAs. But on this day he threw like a top prospect and the number one man in the St. Louis rotation, as the Browns polished off Philadelphia by a final score of 8–2.

On June 12, Roy Mahaffey took the mound against Dick Coffman. The Browns had used all their magic in game one, as the series assumed a more predictable pattern. Mahaffey allowed only four hits to visiting St. Louis while the A's rapped out an even dozen of their own, despite the fact that a couple of the regular starters, most notably Mickey Cochrane, were not in the lineup. Nevertheless, Philadelphia was able to put six runs on the board on the way to the 6–2 victory. More than 30,000 fans crowded into Shibe Park on June 13 to see the doubleheader that would conclude the homestand. Lefty Grove got the start in game one, opposed by Lefty Stewart. Through the first three innings both left-handers traded zeros on the scoreboard, but St. Louis broke through in the top of the fourth to plate the first run of the game. Stewart could not protect the lead for long, however, as he surrendered three runs to the A's in the bottom of the frame. Spotted to a two-run advantage, Grove never looked back. He and the team cruised to a 10–3 win, Grove's eleventh of the season and his second in a row. In the nightcap, George Earnshaw faced Sam Gray in a game that was a laugher from the start.

Philadelphia chased the St. Louis starter in the bottom of the second inning, and by the time the Browns had gotten off the field and back into their own dugout, the A's were on top, 6–0. Adding runs in every inning from the third through the seventh, the team had posted fourteen tallies on the board on the way to a 14–1 pummeling of the Browns. The best hitter at the plate for the hometown heroes this day was once more George Earnshaw. For the second consecutive game, he had gone four-for-five at the dish while hitting the only home run of the contest. Earnshaw was hitting more like a regular position player than a pitcher, and had raised his average to .286 while adding three more RBIs to his season total. More importantly, he had improved his pitching record to 10–2, just one victory short of Grove's club-leading total.

On June 14, the club left the friendly confines of Shibe Park for a road trip that started with a series at Cleveland's League Park against the Indians. Hank McDonald was given the ball for the A's, and his mound opponent was Clint Brown. The Indians struck first with two runs in the bottom of the third, but Philadelphia answered in the top of the fourth, pushing three of their own across to take the lead. When McDonald struggled in the bottom half of the fifth., Bill Shores was brought in to relieve him. Shores was able to retire the Indians without any further scoring, but McDonald had surrendered the tying run. The A's went on top again when they scored in the top of the seventh, but it was Shores who was now unable to hold the lead. To be perfectly fair, it wasn't his fault, but the Indians scored three runs in the bottom of the eighth to take a 6–4 lead. Two Philadelphia errors allowed the Indians batters to have an extended inning, and none of the runs were earned. It was a hard-luck outing for Shores, but he was strapped with the loss in the first game of the road trip.

The second game of the series was played on June 15, and featured

Rube Walberg against Willis Hudlin. Walberg was on top of his game, allowing five hits in his nine innings of work. Though the Tribe managed to score a run, it was unearned, as Philadelphia's vaunted defense booted the ball for its fourth unearned tally in two games. In the meantime, the A's got to Cleveland pitching for four runs, taking the 4–1 victory and improving Walberg's record to 10–2. He and Earnshaw were now just one victory behind Grove. Despite the fact that the A's big three pitchers were all having stellar seasons, Connie Mack continued to search for another quality arm to add to his rotation for the second half of the season. Mack sought to enhance a team already rich in pitching talent, but thus far, he had found no suitable candidates that were available for purchase or trade. As he continued his search, the Philadelphia pitching staff kept on winning games, making it easy for Mack to be selective in making his choice.

June 16 was an off-day for the team, but the A's took the field the following day to complete their three-game series with Cleveland. George Earnshaw took the hill to oppose Wes Ferrell in the rubber game of the series. The A's took the lead early, scoring a run in the bottom of the second inning and adding another in the third. The Indians closed the gap by plating a tally in the top of the fourth, but Philadelphia got the run back in its half of the frame, and went on to post a 4–2 victory. Earnshaw went the distance, allowing only five hits while striking out six Indian batters, and improved his record to 11–2 on the season.

After a travel day on June 18, a well-rested A's team arrived in Chicago to open a series with the White Sox on June 19. Lefty Grove was pitted against Pat Caraway in the opener, which promised to be an easy win for the Mackmen. The final score of 10–4 justified the confidence the team felt in a contest that pitted their ace against Chicago's mediocre pitcher, but the box score showed that it was anything but an easy outing for Grove. Lefty struggled through his nine innings of work, allowing the White Sox 12 hits and a home run. He aided his cause by giving up only one base on balls, however, and made pitches when he had to, inducing six double plays and striking out four. The A's rapped 14 hits of their own, including three home runs, en route to the lopsided victory. Struggle or not, Grove notched another win to run his mark to 12–2 and record his third consecutive victory.

Five. *The Boys of Summer*

On June 20, Rube Walberg took the baseball to face Hal McKain in front of a sparse crowd of approximately 7,500 spectators at Comiskey Park. The A's scored two runs in the top of the first, and for the longest time it appeared as if Walberg was going to make them stand up. Rube held the Sox scoreless through six frames before Chicago finally broke through to score a run in the bottom of the seventh. Philadelphia clung to its 3–1 lead going into the bottom of the ninth, when Luke Appling was sent in to pinch-hit with a Chicago runner on base. Appling delivered a game-tying home run, and the contest went into extra innings. Philadelphia jumped on White Sox reliever Ted Lyons for two runs in the top of the tenth, and Walberg shut down a Chicago rally in the bottom of the frame, allowing just one run to secure the 5–4 win.

Game three of the four-game series featured George Earnshaw against Tommy Thomas. After one inning the A's trailed the Sox, 2–1, but Earnshaw bore down and allowed only one more run in the next seven innings, giving his team a chance to come back. The Mackmen responded, and by the end of the eighth inning held a 6–3 lead in the game. Earnshaw got into trouble in the bottom of the ninth, allowing two runs while recording only one out. Lefty Grove was brought in to relieve Earnshaw, getting the final two outs to earn his fourth save on the season and ensuring that Earnshaw's 12–2 record tied his own.

Bill Shores started the final game of the series at Comiskey Park against Vic Frazier. Both pitchers put goose eggs on the board through the first three innings before the A's broke through to score a run in the top of the fourth. Shores ran into trouble in the bottom of the frame, as the White Sox exploded for five runs before he was able to get the final out. Shores was not to blame, however. All of the runs were unearned, the result of two errors in the field by Max Bishop and Jimmy Dykes. Nevertheless, the A's found themselves trailing by four runs and facing a pitcher that was being stingy in allowing base runners. Frazier scattered six hits while striking out three and allowing no base on balls to stymie the Philadelphia batters. The A's were able to scratch out another run in the top of the seventh, but Chicago answered with three in their half of the inning, as they cruised to an 8–2 win and avoided being swept in the series.

The team moved on to St. Louis to open a five-game series with the

Browns at Sportsman's Park on June 23. It would be a grueling five games in three days that featured doubleheaders on the first and third days, but the team was confident of doing well against the lowly Browns, whose 20–36 record had them 22 games behind the front-running A's, and only a half-game out of last place in the league. Lefty Grove started the first game of the doubleheader slated for June 23, and unlike his previous start, he was in vintage Grove style when he took the mound. The big lefthander threw bullets at the Browns' hitters, allowing only two hits through the course of the game. Grove had to be at his best this day, however, as his mound opponent, Rip Collins, was pitching a gem for the Browns. Collins allowed only one A's run in the top of the second before bearing down to keep any other Philadelphia runners from reaching home plate. It was still a 1–0 game when Browns manager Bill Killefer sent in Rollie Stiles to work in the top of the ninth. Stiles gave up three hits to go along with a free pass, and by the time the Browns were back in the dugout, the A's had scored two insurance runs and were leading, 3–0. Grove took care of business in the bottom of the ninth to earn the complete-game shutout, his thirteenth win on the season and fourth consecutive victory. In the process, he lowered his ERA to a minuscule 1.77.

The second game of the twinbill featured Roy Mahaffey against George Blaeholder. Mahaffey gave up a run in the bottom of the fourth, but the A's tied it up in the top of the fifth. In the bottom of the sixth, Mahaffey ran into trouble, surrendering three runs to give the Browns a 4–1 lead. Philadelphia scratched out another run in the top of the seventh, and Hank McDonald was brought in to pitch in the bottom of the frame. McDonald threw two innings of scoreless ball, giving the team an opportunity to chip away at the two-run lead. In the top of the ninth, the A's pulled even, plating two runs. McDonald gave way to Eddie Rommel, who blanked St. Louis to send the game to extra innings. Chad Kimsey, who had come in to relieve Blaeholder in the top of the ninth, held the A's scoreless in the tenth, eleventh, and twelfth innings, and the Browns won the game in walk-off fashion in the bottom of the twelfth.

Rube Walberg took the mound on June 24. At 11–2, he was trying to keep pace with Grove, and when the A's jumped on St. Louis starter Wally Hebert for two runs in the top of the first inning, it appeared as

Five. The Boys of Summer

if Walberg would have no trouble accomplishing his goal. But Rube surrendered two scores to the Browns in the bottom of the first in a game that would see him bothered by the long ball. St. Louis would hit three home runs against Walberg in five innings of work, two of them coming off the bat of Goose Goslin, and at the end of five frames they would lead, 6–3. Eddie Rommel was brought in to replace Walberg, and his three innings of scoreless work gave the team a chance to come back. Philadelphia did score twice in the top of the seventh to make the contest interesting, but Hebert was able to get the final six outs to earn the 6–5 win.

On June 25, the two teams got together for their second doubleheader in three days. George Earnshaw pitched in the early game against Sam Gray. When the Athletics chased Gray to an early shower with three runs in the top of the second, it looked as if Earnshaw would coast to his thirteenth win of the season. Earnshaw hurled scoreless ball through five innings but was hit hard in the sixth, giving up four runs. The Browns took a 4–3 lead in the game and never looked back. They tacked on two runs in the bottom of the eighth, and held a 6–3 lead when Philadelphia came to the plate in the ninth. The A's made the game interesting, scoring twice in the ninth, but they could not get the tying run across the plate and fell, 6–5. In the nightcap, Billy Shores faced Lefty Stewart. Shores gave up runs in each of the first two innings before Connie Mack put Hank McDonald in the game to replace him in the second. In the meantime, Philadelphia plated three in the top of the second and held a slim 3–2 lead. The A's padded their advantage by scoring a run in the top of the fifth, but then the wheels came off the cart. McDonald gave up three runs in the bottom of the inning before giving way to Eddie Rommel, who was tagged for a run before recording the final out. By the time the smoke cleared, the Browns were ahead, 6–4, and the A's were playing catch-up once more. Rommel gave up two more runs in the bottom of the sixth, and Mack turned to his veteran, Rube Walberg, to stop the bleeding. Walberg pitched scoreless innings in the eighth and ninth, but Philadelphia could not make up the deficit. The team was able to manage only one more run, in the top of the ninth, to lose their fourth game in a row by the score of 8–5. It had been a miserable series in St. Louis. Mack's boys had dropped four out of five games to one of the worst teams in the league, and had allowed the Washington Senators to creep to within one game of the lead in the league standings. Their four-game losing streak was among the longest the team would suffer during the season, as the A's took off a travel day before beginning a series against the Tigers in Detroit.

The best way to stop any losing streak is to send your ace to the mound. Lucky for the A's, June 27 happened to be Lefty Grove's next turn in the rotation to pitch. He faced Art Herring in the series opener. The team spotted Grove to a 3–0 lead after the first half-inning, but the big lefthander was unable to hold it. Grove surrendered two runs in each of the first and second innings, and Philadelphia trailed, 4–3, going into the third. The team pulled even with a run in that frame, and took a 6–4 advantage when two runs came across in the top of the fifth. Although he was touched for a score in the bottom of the fifth, Grove never gave back the lead. The A's tacked on three more in the top of the ninth to take a convincing 9–5 victory, but the game was closer than the final score indicated. Grove surrendered twelve hits and walked five in his nine innings of work while only striking out three. The A's committed three errors behind Lefty to give the Tigers twenty base runners in the game. It wasn't a pretty win, but it was a win nonetheless, and it broke the team's four-game losing streak while extending Grove's personal streak to five.

Of even greater importance to Connie Mack at the time, it gave him an opportunity to evaluate the performance of one of the pitchers he was interested in adding to his staff. Waite Hoyt had come in to pitch in the ninth inning in a relief role. The thirty-one-year-old veteran had been the ace of the Yankees through the 1920s, winning more than 150 games for New York before being sent to Detroit in 1930. Hoyt's record thus far in the 1931 campaign was an unimpressive 3–8, and his earned run average was 5.87, but Mack thought he had the potential to help his team. After fourteen years in the majors, it was assured that he was a veteran who knew his way around a batting lineup, and Mack felt that he still had enough life left in his arm to make him an upgrade over several pitchers he was now sending out to the mound. Negotiations were opened, and on June 30, Philadelphia purchased Hoyt's contract as added insurance for the second half of the season. It would prove to be yet

Five. *The Boys of Summer*

another move of genius made by Mack during the A's days of dominance.

June 28 saw the Athletics playing their third doubleheader in five days. Roy Mahaffey started in the early game against Tommy Bridges. Mahaffey had a touch of wildness, walking six Tiger batters in a complete-game outing, but he allowed only five hits and did not give up an earned run. Detroit scored its lone run in the bottom of the second due to a Jimmy Dykes error. Though the A's had taken an early lead when they scored two in the top of the first, Bridges limited the damage and kept his team in the game through the early going. After five innings of play, the Tigers were still behind by a single run. Then Philadelphia tacked on two more in the top of the sixth and added five in the final two frames to put the game out of reach and record the 9–1 victory. In the second game of the twinbill, Rube Walberg faced George Uhle. The Tigers had been held to a single run in the first game, and they must have felt that their offense was finally getting on track when they scored a run in the bottom of the first to take a 1–0 lead. But that was the only run Walberg gave up in the nightcap, as he limited Detroit to four total hits. The A's tied the game in the top of the fourth, and took a 2–1 lead with a run in the seventh. Dib Williams put an exclamation point on the scoring with a three-run homer in the ninth, and Philadelphia won, 5–1.

Eddie Rommel got a spot start against Earl Whitehill on June 29 in a game that was anything but a pitchers' duel. The two teams combined for twenty-five hits and eleven runs in a wild and wooly affair that saw the Tigers plate the winning run in walk-off fashion in the bottom of the ninth. Jimmie Foxx's fourteenth home run of the season went in a losing cause in this final game of the series at Navin Park. The team did not have much time to think about the loss, however, as they rushed to grab a train for Cleveland, where they were to start the next series of their road trip the following day.

The hit parade that had taken place in Detroit served as a prelude to the offensive explosion that took place in the first game against the Indians on June 30. George Earnshaw climbed the hill to face Clint Brown, and through the early going appeared to have matters well in hand. Cleveland scored first in the bottom of the second, but Philadelphia answered with three in the top of the third. The Indians cut the lead to one with a run in the bottom of the fourth, but the Athletics spoiled their comeback bid by throwing four runs up in the top of the fifth. After the A's added three more insurance runs in the seventh, the game was looking like a laugher with Philadelphia holding a 10–2 lead. Mack's boys ended their scoring with a run in the eighth, and most of the players must have been looking ahead to getting to the clubhouse and deciding where they would go for dinner. But the Indians had other ideas. In the final two frames, Cleveland mounted a rally that made the game interesting, even if it fell short of the victory. By the time the smoke had cleared, the A's held on for an 11–7 win in a game that had twenty-nine hits and thirty-five base runners. Their recent wins had put a little more distance between themselves and the Senators, who now trailed Philadelphia by 3½ games. The Yankees were in third place, twelve games behind, and seemed just about out of the hunt. But in the hot days of July and August, New York would catch fire, while Washington began to melt and slip out of contention.

The second game of the series between the A's and the Indians at League Park on July 1 featured a matchup of team aces, as Lefty Grove toed the rubber against Wes Ferrell. Neither team scored through the first three innings, but Philadelphia broke on top with a run in the top of the fourth. Cleveland answered by pushing one across home plate in the bottom of the inning, and the game remained knotted through five. Both pitchers were giving the opposition scoring chances, with each hurler allowing eleven hits in the course of the contest, but they were able to eliminate any possible damage by inducing batters to hit into double plays. Each team hit into three twin killings, which erased potential scoring threats and kept the game close. The A's scored two in the top of the sixth, and with Grove throwing heat, looked to have the game in the bag. But Cleveland rallied for two of their own in the bottom of the seventh to deadlock the contest. The tie was short-lived, as Philadelphia got to Ferrell for another run in the top of the eighth, and Lefty shut the door through the final two frames to earn the 4–3 victory and run his winning streak to six games. With a little more than half the season still to be played, Grove had already amassed fifteen wins.

By July, the hitting woes that had plagued the team in the spring

FIVE. *The Boys of Summer*

Hall of Fame catcher Mickey Cochrane, who served as the team captain of the Athletics. Cochrane's fiery, competitive spirit matched his prowess both behind and at the plate, making him one of the all-time best backstops in the game.

were long-forgotten. Al Simmons and Mickey Cochrane had cooled off a little in recent weeks, but they were still hitting .370 and .358, respectively. Bing Miller had improved his average to .282, and Max Bishop, Jimmie Foxx and Jimmy Dykes were all hitting .290 or better. The most pleasant surprise of these early days of summer was Mule Haas. The A's regular center fielder was having the best year of his career thus far at the plate, batting .331. He was also providing yet another power threat for the club, as evidenced by the two doubles he swatted in the July 1 game against the Indians. With seven starters averaging .282 or better and with the home run threat posed by Cochrane, Foxx, and Simmons, the A's lineup presented a formidable threat to any opposing pitcher. The team could win the close ones with their own great pitching, or they could go toe-to-toe in a slugfest. With all parts of the game coming together, it was hard to imagine that any team could catch the A's, and most baseball fans merely speculated on who would finish second in the league for the season.

On July 2, Rube Walberg took his 12–3 record to the mound to face Cleveland's Willis Hudlin. Though Grove's torrid pace was putting distance between himself and Walberg, Rube was still ranked among the pitching leaders in the league. The A's took the lead early when they scored four runs in the top of the second. Jimmie Foxx started things off with a solo home run. Bing Miller and Jimmy Dykes made outs before Dib Williams got a hit, and was followed by a walk to Walberg. Max Bishop then stepped to the plate and hammered a three-run homer, and the A's were off and running. But that was all the scoring the team was to do this day. Though Hudlin would give up thirteen hits throughout the game, he was able to strand all successive Philadelphia base runners. In the meantime, the Indians started chipping away at the Athletics' lead. They scored two in the bottom of the third to cut the lead in half, then exploded in the sixth to take a commanding lead. Walberg couldn't seem to get anyone out in the sixth inning as the Indians batted around, scoring six runs while only making one out. Earnshaw came in to relieve Walberg, and though he did record the final two outs, he gave up another run. Earl Averill proved to be particularly troublesome to both Walberg and Earnshaw by hitting a home run off each pitcher. Cleveland added three more runs in the bottom of the seventh off reliever Lew Krausse,

Five. *The Boys of Summer*

and the Athletics went quietly in the final two frames to the 12–4 beating. Lopsided wins were usually in the favor of Philadelphia, but not on this day when neither the pitching nor the hitting seemed to be able to get on track.

July 3 was a travel day for the team. The A's would be in Philadelphia to celebrate the Fourth of July holiday as they opened a short one-day series in Shibe Park with the Red Sox. The fans would get their money's worth, though, as the brief homestand consisted of a doubleheader Attendance was far less than Mack hoped for when his team returned to the friendly confines of Shibe Park. The fact that Boston was struggling and more than twenty games off the pace could have kept some fans away, but it was more likely that the continuing effects of the Depression were to blame. Regardless of the reason, there were many empty seats in the stadium once the Philadelphia faithful came through the turnstiles to root on their first-place A's that holiday afternoon.

Roy Mahaffey opposed Ed Morris in the first game and was staked to a seven-run lead as the Philadelphia bats exploded in the bottom of the first inning. The power strokes and timely hitting that had been absent in the last game in Cleveland were once again on display. Morris never made it out of the first inning, and the Red Sox used four pitchers on a day that would see the A's club four doubles, a triple, and a homer by Dib Williams for good measure. Mahaffey couldn't take advantage of his good fortune, as he was tagged for four runs in the top of the second, leaving the game after just 1⅓ innings pitched. Eddie Rommel came in to get the final two outs of the frame before handing the ball over to Lefty Grove to start the top of the third. Grove struck out ten Red Sox batters over the next seven innings but also gave up three runs. Philadelphia added two more scores in the later innings to escape with the 9–7 victory and earn Grove his seventh consecutive win. Lefty was now 16–2, but the three runs allowed in this game caused his ERA to "balloon" to 2.13, still best in the league by far.

The nightcap featured Waite Hoyt getting his first Philadelphia start against Wilcy Moore. Waite's record thus far in the season with Detroit had been 3–8, but his fortunes were about to change with his new club. Most of the game was a pitchers' duel, and at the end of seven full innings the score was tied, 2–2. In the bottom of the eighth, the A's bats finally came to life as the team plated four runs to give Hoyt a comfortable advantage. Jimmie Foxx had a big day in the batter's box, going three-for-four. Al Simmons had only one hit in his four plate appearances but drove in two and scored a run. But the best day with a bat was possibly reserved for Hoyt, who went two-for-two with a sacrifice, drove in one, and scored one. It was an auspicious start for the 31-year-old veteran Connie Mack thought could help his club, and it was providential that the victory put the A's thirty-one games over .500 with a record of 51–20.

July 5 saw the team at Griffith Stadium in Washington to open an important series against the Senators. Washington was 5½ games behind in the standings, and hoped to make up some ground in the five-game set. George Earnshaw got the starting assignment against Firpo Marberry and had an early 1–0 lead when he pitched in the bottom of the first. Washington got to the hard-throwing Earnshaw for two runs in the third and fourth innings, taking a 4–1 lead in the game. Only one of the scores was earned, however, as four Philadelphia errors contributed to the scoring. For their part, the A's were able to get to Marberry for only one more run, scored in the visiting half of the sixth, and a fine pitching performance by Earnshaw was wasted in a 4–2 loss.

Rube Walberg faced Bump Hadley in the second game of the series on July 6. In a classic pitchers' duel, neither team was able to plate a run through eight innings of play. The efforts of both starting pitchers went for naught when the scoreless contest had to be called due to inclement weather. The two teams faced off again on July 7 with George Earnshaw slated to go against General Crowder. Earnshaw allowed eight hits and three runs in nine innings of work, which was good enough for him to collect his 14th victory on the year. The A's batters rapped ten hits, seven of them for extra bases, including five double and two triples, accounting for seven runs and a 7–3 win. Philadelphia's lead was back to 5½ games.

It was Lefty Grove's turn in the rotation when the two teams met for the next game of the series on July 8. Washington sent Lloyd Brown to the mound to oppose him, but Brown got into trouble right from the start, surrendering four runs in the top of the first that gave Grove a lead he would never relinquish. The big bats of the Philadelphia lineup would shine on this day, with the exception of Mickey Cochrane, who

Five. The Boys of Summer

had an uncharacteristic zero-for-four at the plate. Mule Haas went two-for-five with a triple, while Simmons and Foxx each went two-for-four. Simmons belted a double and a triple, while Foxx took Brown deep with a long ball, his sixteenth of the season. Lefty coasted to a 6–3 win, allowing only two earned runs in nine innings. The streak now stood at eight, and people were taking notice, even if no one was considering him to be a serious challenger to the record. What was more important to Connie Mack and most people who followed the game was that the Senators had lost another game in the standings and possibly their best chance to get back into the race for a pennant.

Philadelphia continued its road trip to New York to face the Yankees on July 9. The players must have felt like a troupe of homeless vagabonds as they arrived in the big city to face their archrivals. The team had undertaken a lengthy road trip that had taken the A's to Chicago, St. Louis, Detroit and Cleveland, and had been back home in Philadelphia only for a single day before packing their bags for another long stint away from Shibe Park. They had gone 10–5 on the previous trip, and were thus far 2–1 on a nine-game road trip that would see them playing the role of visiting team on all but one day from June 19 to July 12. For three and one-half weeks the A's dealt with the grind of trains, buses, hotel rooms, and hostile crowds as they battled opposing teams that always had the last at-bat. During this period they would amass a record of 17–8, proving themselves to be road warriors as dangerous away from Shibe Park as they were within its friendly confines. The only team that had given them serious problems during this stretch had been the lowly Browns. When the games mattered against anyone in possible contention for the pennant, the team had come through. Now they were facing the Yankees, and while they held a comfortable eleven-game lead over their third-place rivals, everyone knew that the Yanks had been heating up and were a dangerous foe on the field.

Hank McDonald got the start in a brief one-game series at Yankee Stadium on July 11. He was opposed by future Hall of Famer Red Ruffing in one of the best-pitched games of the summer. The A's jumped out to a 1–0 lead when Al Simmons drove in Joe Palmisano, who was doing the catching duties behind the plate to give Mickey Cochrane a day off and stroked a two-out double to get in scoring position. But that was all the scoring the A's were to do that day. Ruffing shut the door tight, allowing only two more hits the rest of the way while striking out eight and walking none. McDonald also was extremely stingy in allowing hits, giving up only two in seven innings of work. He did walk three, however, and both hits and one of the walks came back to haunt him. Both Yankee batters to hit their way on base did so with home runs. Lou Gehrig swatted a two-run shot in the fourth, and Jimmie Reese added a solo homer in the fifth to give Ruffing all the run support he would need on his way to the 3–1 victory. It was a hard-luck loss for McDonald, who had pitched his heart out and made only two mistakes on the day. Unfortunately for him, both of his mistakes left the yard.

Following the loss, the road-weary A's packed their bags and made their way to Boston, where they took on the Red Sox at Braves Stadium on July 12. Waite Hoyt started the first game of a scheduled doubleheader against Wilcy Moore, the same pitcher he had faced in the July 4 doubleheader in Philadelphia. The A's got to Moore in the top of the first for two runs, then chased him in the fifth when they erupted for five scores, capped by solo home runs by Al Simmons and Jimmie Foxx. That was more than enough cushion for Hoyt, who allowed only six hits to Red Sox batters and gave up a single earned run in nine innings. The final score was 7–2, and if there was any part of the Athletics' game that could stand some improvement, it was their propensity for allowing unearned runs to opponents. Game two of the twinbill featured Roy Mahaffey against Ed Morris. The A's struck early, as was beginning to become a trademark with the team, and Mahaffey took the mound to pitch in the bottom of the second spotted to a 2–0 lead. The Athletics went on to tack on runs in each of the fourth, fifth and sixth innings, and going into the bottom of the sixth, Mahaffey had a comfortable 6–0 lead. Boston tried to stage a comeback when Earl Webb hit a home run with a man aboard, but that was as close as the Red Sox could get. The game was called after six innings of play due to unfavorable conditions and Philadelphia was awarded the 6–2 win. The Philadelphia "travel team" was at last headed back to the City of Brotherly Love to open an extended homestand.

The A's were on top in their league and had the best record in baseball, but Connie Mack still had reason for concern as the team returned

Five. The Boys of Summer

home. Financial considerations were occupying more of his attention as the owner-manager tried to cope with the ever-decreasing gate revenue coming from ticket sales. Philadelphia had the highest payroll in baseball, and was still making payments on Shibe Park. The Great Depression had stopped the banks from advancing credit, so the team had to try to keep itself afloat with the cash it generated from ticket sales. Mack acknowledged that the declining ticket sales were in part due to the poor economy, and a need for fans to be more frugal with their spending, but he also contemplated that there might be another reason why the Philadelphia faithful were not coming out to support their team in large numbers. "Our Philadelphia fans are unlike those in New York," he stated. "It is a curious fact, demonstrated over and over again that Philadelphians will turn out in greater numbers to see their home team fight to become champions than they will to see them fight to remain champions."[4] If Mack was right, one of the best baseball teams ever to play the game was suffering from its own success in this, their third successive year of dominance in the game. Whatever the reason, the A's success on the diamond was not translating into a financial gain for the team owners, who viewed the future with both hope and apprehension.

Six

Dog Days and Another Winning Streak

The Athletics returned to Philadelphia with a little more than half of the regular season completed. They opened the homestand with a doubleheader against the Washington Senators, who were still only five games back and within striking distance of catching the A's. Lefty Grove got the ball in game one of the twinbill, opposed by Bump Hadley. The stands were unusually full to welcome the A's return to the city, and more than 35,000 turned out to see the games, many of them undoubtedly coming to see if Lefty could extend his streak. Grove's first-half record of 17–2 was best in the majors, and the left-handed fireballer was generally regarded as being the best current pitcher in the game. Grove's fastball was what legends are made of. He was the hardest thrower of his era, and is regarded by many to have been the fastest of all time. A story is told of Walter "The Big Train" Johnson going to see Bob Feller pitch when "Rapid Robert" was the new phenom of the game. A Washington sports reporter, who referred to Johnson as "the most modest man you would ever know," said that the Hall of Fame great watched Feller throw for a couple innings, remarking, "Oh, he's fast!" and a little later, "Oh, my! He's fast!" When asked if Feller threw as fast as he did in his prime, Johnson replied, "No, and I don't think he's as fast as Lefty Grove." Lefty lived and died with his fastball. When he got two strikes on a batter, he usually went to his out pitch, which was a letter-high heater that rose out of the strike zone as it crossed the plate. A batter who faced Grove commented, "If you took it, it would be a ball. But if you had two strikes on you, you couldn't take it. It was that close and he had great control."[1] Grove was definitely the best of his time, having

Six. Dog Days and Another Winning Streak

both speed and control, but he also needed another key ingredient if he hoped to extend his consecutive games winning streak: luck. When he took the mound to face Washington in game one of the doubleheader he was about to get his fair share of that, and then some.

In what was becoming a trademark, the A's scored first in their half of the opening frame, staking Grove to a 3-0 lead. It was not enough. Lefty did not have his best stuff this day, and he was not picked up by his teammates in the field. Grove allowed thirteen hits to Senators batters and gave up seven runs. To be sure, only two of the runs were earned, the other five coming as a result of four Philadelphia errors, but when Grove exited the game after eight innings of work, he was trailing, 7-5, and it looked as if his streak was about to end. When the A's came to the plate in the bottom of the eighth, they were seeking to make atonement with their bats for a sloppy performance in the field. Firpo Marberry had started the game for the Senators and surrendered five runs through seven innings of work. Bump Hadley replaced him in the eighth, and everything began to unravel for Washington. Hadley did not record an out while giving up a hit and three walks. The score was 7-6 when Bobby Burke was brought in with the bases loaded and nobody out to face Dib Williams. Williams, pinch-hitting for Grove, went yard for a grand slam that put Philadelphia on top again. Al Simmons later belted a two-out solo shot off Burke to cap a seven-run outburst that gave the A's a 12-7 lead. George Earnshaw came in to pitch the ninth and shut the door on the Senators, securing the win and keeping Grove's consecutive streak alive. Lefty was now 18-2, and he was more than halfway toward tying the American League record for successive victories.

Rube Walberg faced General Crowder in the nightcap. As usual, the A's struck first, even if it did take them until the bottom of the third inning to do so. Walberg took a 1-0 lead to the top of the fourth, but the Senators answered with two of their own, taking a 2-1 advantage. Philadelphia pulled even with a run in the bottom of the frame, but that was as close as they would get in this game. Washington plated four in the sixth on a day that would see Walberg become susceptible to the long ball, giving up homers to Dave Harris and Joe Kuhel. Philadelphia tried to rally in the later innings, scoring two runs in the eighth, but came up short in the 6–4 loss. The split meant that Washington was still five games back in the standings when the Senators left town.

The Tigers came to Philadelphia to open a series on July 14 that featured George Earnshaw against Art Herring in the opener. Earnshaw was given the ball even though he had pitched in relief for Grove in game one of the doubleheader the previous day. It is impossible to know if Earnshaw was just having an off-day or if he was tired when he took the mound, but it is certain that his outing resulted in a slaughter. The Tigers scored early and often, and by the end of three innings held a 5–1 lead. By the time eight full innings were in the books, Detroit had touched Earnshaw for eight runs on eleven hits and held an 8–3 lead. Jim Peterson was brought in to relieve Earnshaw in the top of the ninth, but he had even less luck with the Tigers' batters than the starter. Detroit clubbed Peterson for four runs on five hits and a walk, and the A's went quietly in their half of the inning to take a 12–3 drubbing.

July 15 featured yet another doubleheader in the July heat of Philadelphia. Waite Hoyt got the start in the first game against Tommy Bridges. Hoyt was unbeaten since joining the A's, and though his modest two-game streak did not compare with Grove's, he was looking to extend his own winning ways as long as he could. Roy Johnson opened with a hit for the Tigers to start the first inning, and was followed by Charlie Gehringer, who made Hoyt pay with a two-run homer. The A's plated two of their own in the bottom of the second to pull even, but Detroit scratched out a go-ahead run in the top of the third. Both pitchers settled in to put zeros on the board through the middle innings as the bats for each team went silent. Hoyt held the Tigers to eight hits in the contest. Bridges limited Philadelphia to only five hits, but a touch of wildness gave the A's another seven base runners on walks. In the bottom of the eighth, Philadelphia was able to cluster its limited number of hits and walks to push three runners across home plate and take a 5–3 lead. Hoyt finished off the ninth to keep his undefeated record with the A's intact and win his third in a row.

Game two of the twinbill was not nearly so dramatic. Hank McDonald was on the mound for the Athletics, opposed by Earl Whitehill. McDonald had pitched so well in his last outing against New York, throwing a two-hit complete game. Unfortunately, both hits had been

Six. Dog Days and Another Winning Streak

home runs, resulting in three scores for the Yankees and giving McDonald a hark-luck loss. This game was different. There would be no hard luck to spoil McDonald's efforts, and he would leave no mistakes out over the plate to be hit over the Shibe Park fence. He would also get plenty of run support from his teammates. The A's took the lead in the first, getting to Whitehill for three early runs. Mule Haas then belted a three-run blast in the second that gave McDonald a comfortable 6–0 lead and sent Whitehill to the showers after getting only six outs. Philadelphia would add single runs off Charlie Sullivan, the Detroit reliever, in both the fourth and seventh innings, and would cap the scoring when Al Simmons cleared the fence with a three-run homer in the bottom of the eighth. In the meantime, McDonald frustrated Tiger hitters all afternoon, allowing only three hits and two walks in nine innings of work to earn an 11–0 shutout victory.

Roy Mahaffey opposed Vic Sorrell in the third game of the four-game set on July 16. The Tigers struck first when Charlie Gehringer, John Stone, and Dale Alexander reached base in the top of the third. Marty McManus then brought them home with a bases-clearing double, and the A's were behind, 3–0. Philadelphia scored one in the fourth and three in the fifth to take a 4–3 lead. Mahaffey helped his own cause by hitting a solo home run in the sixth to close out the Athletics' scoring. He then held on to shut out Detroit for the final three frames and earn the 5–3 win. Mahaffey was not one of the pitchers that came to mind when one thought about the stars on the Philadelphia staff, but he had quietly compiled a respectable 8–2 record, and was proving himself a complementary addition to the big three on the staff.

Lefty Grove would make his bid for a tenth straight win when he took the mound in the final game of the series with Detroit, facing George Uhle. The A's started him out on the right foot by scoring four runs in the bottom of the second. Grove, meanwhile, blanked the Tigers through the first five innings of play. Detroit finally got on the board in the top of the sixth but still trailed, 4–1. Insurance runs in the seventh and eighth innings increased Philadelphia's lead to 6–1, and with only three outs left to go, the Tigers faced an almost impossible challenge. But a Max Bishop error gave new life to Detroit and led to two unearned runs, but that was all Grove would allow. The 6–3 final kept Lefty's streak

Lefty Grove and the 1931 Philadelphia Athletics

Lefty Grove, the left-handed flamethrower who served as the pitching ace of the Philadelphia Athletics during their dynasty years in the late 1920s and early 1930s. Grove is considered by many to have been the best to ever play the game at his position.

Six. Dog Days and Another Winning Streak

going. He was as hot as the weather, and had just notched his tenth victory in a row. The team won its fourth straight and was on its way to another streak.

The White Sox came to town on July 18 to become the next victims of the surging A's. George Earnshaw faced Red Faber in the first game of the series. The game was a merry-go-round on the base paths, as the teams combined for thirty-two hits, with nine walks and two more batters reaching base through errors. Earnshaw went a full nine innings before departing the game, trailing, 5–3. Faber was chased in the bottom of the ninth, charged with two runs while recording just one out. Vic Frazier came in to close out the inning, but the damage had been done. With the score tied, 5–5, the game went into extra frames. Eddie Rommel took over the pitching duties for the A's in the top of the tenth and blanked Chicago in its half of the inning. Frazier returned the favor when Philadelphia came to bat, and the game moved on to the eleventh. Rommel faltered in the eleventh when the Sox scored a run to take a 6–5 lead. His teammates got him off the hook, however, with another late-inning rally. Frazier was chased from the game with two runners on in the bottom of the eleventh after recording only a single out. Pat Caraway came in to replace him but walked the only man he faced to load the bases. Chicago manager Donie Bush then turned to Tommy Thomas to get him out of the bases-loaded jam. Thomas had trouble finding the strike zone, however, walking in two runs to give the Athletics a 7–6 victory. It wasn't pretty, but a win was a win, and it was the fifth in a row for the team.

Rube Walberg started the second game of the series against Pat Caraway on July 18. Caraway had a rough outing the previous day, unable to get an out in his relief appearance for Frazier. The situation did not improve for him after a night of rest. Caraway was rocked in the first inning for five runs. With one out, Mule Haas got a pitch he could handle and deposited it over the fence at Shibe Park. The hit parade then began, as the A's plated four more runs before picking up their gloves to take the field again. Walberg gave up one in the top of the second, but the A's got it back off reliever Vic Frazier when they came to bat. Frazier held Philadelphia scoreless for the next three innings before giving up another score in the sixth. Walberg gave that run back in the top of the seventh but then slammed the door to earn the 7–2 complete-game victory. In a summer of streaks within streaks, the team had won its sixth consecutive game, and was now 7½ games in front of second-place Washington.

Hank McDonald started the third game of the series with the White Sox on July 20. His mound opponent was Tommy Thomas. McDonald had pitched a shutout against the Tigers a few days before, but he ran into trouble early in this outing, even though most of it was not of his making. Chicago center fielder Lu Blue led off the game by reaching base on an error on Joe Boley. McDonald was trying to hold Blue close but balked, sending the base runner to second. Billy Sullivan connected for a single, and the Sox had runners on first and third with no outs. Carl Reynolds hit a ball that Max Bishop bobbled, scoring Blue. Lew Fonseca singled to load the bases. Johnny Watwood then singled to bring in Sullivan. The bases were still loaded when John Kerr hit a fly ball to right field that was deep enough to bring Reynolds home. Bill Cissell flied out to left, and with two outs it looked as if McDonald was going to have a chance to get out of the nightmare inning. Frank Grube was at the plate, a sub-.200 hitter that should have been an easy out, but McDonald was flustered. He threw a wild pitch to Grube that allowed Fonseca and Watwood to advance, then walked Grube to load the bases again. Tommy Thomas came to the plate for what should have been the third out of the inning, but the White Sox attempted the incredible. They tried a triple steal that ended up succeeding, as Fonseca stole home and Grube and Watwood both advanced. McDonald was obviously unnerved by the whole affair, and proceeded to give up a single to his mound opponent that drove in two. Blue came up for his second time in the inning and grounded a ball to Jimmie Foxx that the first baseman took unassisted to finally end the comedy of errors and get Philadelphia off the field. Chicago had scored six runs in its half of the first, none of them earned, as errors in the field continued to plague the A's in what was beginning to emerge as an Achilles' heel.

When Thomas took the mound in the bottom of the inning, it appeared as if the two pitchers had reversed the fortunes of their previous outings. Thomas couldn't get anyone out two days earlier when he had come in as a reliever against the Athletics. Max Bishop led off

Six. Dog Days and Another Winning Streak

with a double, but Thomas got Haas and Cochrane to ground out. Bishop scored on Cochrane's ground out. Al Simmons then singled, but Jimmie Foxx grounded out to end the inning. Chicago led, 6–1, and things did not look good for Philadelphia. When they took the field again, Roy Mahaffey replaced the shell-shocked McDonald. Mahaffey sat the White Sox down in order, however, and the A's went to the bat rack to try to get back in the game.

The White Sox did all they could to repay the gifts they had been given earlier by the A's. Bing Miller led off the inning by popping out to the shortstop. Jimmy Dykes reached second on a two-base error by Watwood, and moved to third when Joe Boley singled. Mahaffey came up and helped his own cause by rapping a single that scored Dykes. Max Bishop struck out, which should have been the third out of the inning, but Watwood's earlier error allowed play to continue. Haas and Cochrane then singled, driving in Boley and Mahaffey. Simmons followed with the third straight single, bringing Haas in to score. That was the end of the day for Thomas. Pat Caraway was brought in to relieve him and face Jimmie Foxx. But the Sox were not done imitating the Keystone Kops act they had seen in the first inning. Foxx reached base on an error to Cissell, which scored Cochrane. Bing Miller popped out to second to mercifully end the inning. Philadelphia had put five runs on the scoreboard, all of them unearned, and had tied the game, 6–6.

The third inning proved to be boring, considering what had already taken place. The White Sox were retired in order in their half of the inning, and Philadelphia went quietly in its part of the frame with a single base on balls. In the bottom of the fourth, Mule Haas led off with a home run that cleared the fence. Two outs later, Jimmie Foxx hit a ball to center field that ended up being a home run of the inside-the-park variety, and the A's took an 8–6 lead.

Foxx must have been winded by his race around the base path, as he committed an error on a ball hit by Chicago's leadoff hitter in the fifth, Lew Fonseca. By the time the play was over, Fonseca was standing on second with nobody out. Two batters later, John Kerr's single brought Fonseca home with yet another unearned run to make the game a single-score affair.

In the bottom of the sixth, Max Bishop struck out, followed by

Haas, who singled. Mickey Cochrane struck out, and it looked like Caraway was going to have an easy inning. But the middle of the Philadelphia batting order was at the bat rack, and they intended to do some damage. Al Simmons singled, and Caraway pitched carefully to Foxx, walking him instead of giving in and throwing one the big righthander could hit. Bing Miller made him pay by rapping a triple that cleared the bases and sent Caraway to the showers. Jim Moore came in to get the final out of the inning, but the A's now had an 11–7 lead. An insurance run in the bottom of the seventh ended the scoring for the day for the A's, and Mahaffey blanked the White Sox in their final two at-bats to earn the 12–7 victory in one of the most bizarre games of the year. Philadelphia pitching had given up seven runs on eight its, but all of the runs were unearned. The A's had also scored five unearned runs, as neither team seemed able to catch and throw the ball correctly. In any streak, there must be a certain element of good fortune. There are times when Lady Luck can be prevailed upon to bestow her favors, and there are times when she insists that you earn the luck that comes your way. In the case of the July 20 game against the White Sox, the A's experienced dumb luck, where they did everything wrong and still managed to emerge victorious. A too-frequent tendency to boot the ball in the field must have driven Connie Mack to distraction. His team had enough talent and experience to overcome some errors in the field, but Mack must have known that sloppy play would eventually cost the team a game when it really counted. For the moment, everyone was satisfied to log the team's seventh straight win.

The final game of the series with Chicago was played on July 21, with the rejuvenated Waite Hoyt taking the mound to face Vic Frazier. Hoyt benefited from another Chicago error in the bottom of the second that resulted in five A's crossing home plate, four of them after what should have been the final out. Philadelphia gave three runs back to the Sox in the top of the third, before Hoyt clamped down to pitch four scoreless innings. Hal McKain came in to replace Frazier in the bottom of the seventh, and the A's greeted him rudely. Two walks, two hits, and an error later, McKain had given up three runs. Doc Cramer had pinch-hit for Hoyt during the rally, so George Earnshaw came into the game to try to close things out versus the Sox. He gave up two runs in his first

Six. Dog Days and Another Winning Streak

inning of work, then settled down to retire Chicago in order in the ninth, earning a save for himself and Hoyt's fourth consecutive victory. It was also the eighth straight in a healthy winning streak the team was putting together as it looked toward the end of July.

The Cleveland Indians brought their .500 record to Shibe Park on July 22 to open a five-game series with the A's. Rube Walberg took his start in the rotation against Mel Harder. The Indians manufactured two runs on a walk and three hits and led the game, 2–0, going into the bottom of the first. Al Simmons doubled in a run in the A's half of the frame to cut the Cleveland lead in half. A Cochrane RBI in the bottom of the second evened the score until the bottom of the fifth, when Miller, who had doubled, scored on an error by Luke Sewell. An Earl Averill home run in the top of the sixth knotted things up again, but Philadelphia blew the game open in the bottom of the seventh with a four-run flurry. Simmons started the hit parade with a double to left and came home on a single by Foxx. Bing Miller singled, as did Eric McNair, and the bases were loaded with one out. Dib Williams tripled to center, clearing the bases, and the A's took a 7–3 lead. Walberg allowed one hit in the final two innings to secure his fourteenth win of the season and the ninth win in a row for the team.

George Earnshaw started the second game of the series with Willis Hudlin as his mound opponent. Earnshaw was on his game, sitting the Indians down in order in the top of the first. In the bottom of the inning, the Athletics put three runs on the scoreboard, powered by the two-run homer by Mickey Cochrane. In their next at bat, Al Simmons singled home Max Bishop to make it a 4–0 lead. That was more than enough run support for Earnshaw, who was throwing a beauty from the mound. George scattered five hits through the course of the game and struck out six Indians batters while issuing only one base on balls and a hit batter. Two of the Cleveland hits came in the eighth, along with the base on balls and the hit batter. It accounted for two Indian runs and was the only real trouble Earnshaw got into during his nine innings. The result was a 5–2 victory for Earnshaw, his sixteenth on the season, and the team's win streak was extended to ten.

Roy Mahaffey, with a personal winning streak of his own, started the third game of the series on July 24. Clint Brown took the ball for the

Tribe in a low-scoring pitchers' duel in front of the Philadelphia faithful. Mahaffey walked two of the first three batters he faced in the opening inning, then gave up an RBI single to Joe Vosmik to give Cleveland the lead. But that was about all of the offensive production the Indians would muster on this day. Mahaffey would bear down to allow only one more walk and two more hits the rest of the day, as he sat down the Indian batters in rapid succession. Harder was having a good outing himself. In the bottom of the second, Bing Miller got a two-out double, then came home on a McNair single to tie the game. McNair ended up on third due to an error on Montague, and was driven in by a Dib Williams double. That was all the offensive production the A's would be able to muster. Harder scattered five more hits during the rest of his outing while holding the A's scoreless in the remaining innings. The game was called for inclement weather after the sixth inning. Mahaffey got the victory, running his record to 10–2. Not bad for a pitcher who was fourth or fifth on the depth chart. The team streak now stood at eleven, and with Lefty Grove scheduled to pitch the following day, there was no reason to think it would not continue to an even dozen.

Wes Ferrell got the nod from Cleveland skipper Roger Peckinpaugh to take the mound for the Indians against Lefty Grove in the first game of a doubleheader on July 25. Ferrell was having a good season, owning a record of 13–8, and as with most competitive athletes, probably welcomed the chance to face the pitcher hailed as the best in the game.

One hit and two walks was the combined offense generated by both teams through the first two innings. In the top of the third, Ed Montague led off the inning with a double, and advanced to third on a ground out by Ferrell. Bob Seeds singled to center to bring Montague home, and the Indians led, 1–0. The A's got back into the game in the bottom of the fourth when Simmons led off with a single. Jimmie Foxx walked, and Bing Miller then laid down a sacrifice bunt that moved Simmons and Foxx ninety feet up the base paths. McNair grounded out to third, allowing Simmons to score and tie the game. Dib Williams received an intentional walk to get to Grove, who was not known to swing the bat particularly well. But Lefty made Ferrell pay for the free pass to Williams by slapping a single that plated Foxx and gave Philadelphia the lead. The Indians regained the advantage in the top of the sixth when Cleveland

Six. Dog Days and Another Winning Streak

strung together three singles that led to two runs. The Athletics took control of the game in the seventh, driving three runs across the plate to take the lead for good. An insurance run was added in the eighth, and Grove did the rest, blanking the Indians through the final three innings to earn the 6–3 win, his eleventh in a row and the twelfth straight for the team.

The nightcap featured Hank McDonald opposing Sarge Connally. It was a tough start for Connally, who had been out of baseball the previous season and was trying to earn a spot with the Tribe. The A's were hot, and the Philadelphia faithful had turned out in relatively large numbers to take in the doubleheader this day, giving Connally a hostile crowd to deal with, as well as a fearsome lineup. Connally got off to a rough start when he walked the leadoff man, Max Bishop, then surrendered a double to Mule Haas that scored the first run of the game with no outs. But Connally settled down to induce the next two batters into ground outs, and struck out Jimmie Foxx to end the inning with no further damage being done. Both pitchers then began putting zeros on the scoreboard for the next six innings, as the batters for each team were stymied. In the top of the eighth, the A's malady struck again when Jimmie Foxx misplayed a ball that led to Cleveland scoring two unearned runs to take a 2–1 lead. In the top of the ninth, McDonald got a fly out, then gave up a hit and a walk before being replaced by Rube Walberg. Walberg induced an inning-ending double play, and the A's went to the bottom of the ninth needing a run to keep their streak alive.

Mickey Cochrane led off with a double, and Phil Todt pinch-hit for Walberg. Todt laid down a bunt to advance Cochrane but reached first safely on a fielder's choice when the Indians tried to get the lead man. Max Bishop came to the plate with the potential tying run on third but struck out. Mule Haas picked up Bishop by rapping a single to right that brought Cochrane home and moved Todt to third. Dib Williams followed and slapped another single to right that proved to be the game-winner, giving Walberg the 3–2 victory and improving his record to 15–5. It was the thirteenth consecutive win for the team and nicely complemented the seventeen-game stretch the A's had put together earlier in the season. With a .737 winning percentage, the Athletics had the best record in baseball, and led second-place Washington by a full eleven games. This victory came with a price, however. Mule Haas fractured a wrist that would keep his hot bat out of the lineup for the next several weeks.[2] Doc Cramer and Jimmy Moore would platoon in center field to replace him until his injury had healed and he was sufficiently ready to play.

The Athletics and Indians continued their matchup on July 26, but they did so at League Park in Cleveland. Waite Hoyt faced Mel Harder in the sixth game of this home-and-home series, which was a short one-game set. Hoyt took a personal winning streak of four games to the mound with him, but the success he had thus far experienced in a Philadelphia uniform would fail him this day against the Indians. Through six innings of work, Hoyt gave up four walks and surrendered fifteen hits, leading to ten runs. Eddie Rommel was brought in to replace him in the seventh, but Rommel could not stop the bleeding. He allowed three walks and four hits that led to three more Indian runs, as the best pitching staff in the majors got hammered for more than a dozen scores. Harder, in the meantime, kept the A's batters off-balance by scattering nine hits and giving up single runs in the fourth and seventh innings. Ironically, the thirteen-game winning streak of the A's was ended by a thirteen-run Indian offensive explosion. Hoyt's stretch had come to a close as well, as the veteran hurler fell to two games below .500 with a record of 7–9.

With the one-day foray to Cleveland ended, the A's returned home to Shibe Park to open a series with the Browns. Rube Walberg faced off against George Blaeholder in game one. Philadelphia jumped out to an early lead in the bottom of the first when Cochrane and Simmons both tripled and Foxx reached base on an error, bringing Simmons in. St. Louis pulled even in the top of the fourth on two singles and a double. A solo home run by Bing Miller in the bottom of the seventh gave the Athletics the lead, but Walberg served up a two-run shot to Fred Schulte in the top of the eighth to leave Philadelphia trailing, 4–3. Doc Cramer doubled to lead off the A's half of the ninth inning, then came in to score on a single by Al Simmons. With the score knotted at 4–4, the game went to extra innings. Both starting pitchers were still on the mound. Walberg gave up a leadoff single in the top of the tenth before retiring the next three batters in order. Blaeholder recorded the first out of the bottom of the frame before Eric McNair came to the plate. McNair got

Six. Dog Days and Another Winning Streak

a pitch he could handle, driving it over the fence for a walk-off home run that gave the Athletics a 5–4 victory.

Game two of the series featured George Earnshaw pitted against Wally Hebert. The A's used two walks and two St. Louis errors to manufacture a run in the bottom of the first to take an early lead, and tacked on another score in the fifth to put the Browns in a 2–0 hole. St. Louis cut the deficit in half in the top of the seventh, then chased Earnshaw in the eighth when Goose Goslin belted a two-run homer with nobody out. Lefty Grove came in to relieve Earnshaw, and retired the Browns in order. Al Simmons led off the bottom of the eighth with a home run that tied the score. Jimmie Foxx walked, and Bing Miller doubled to left to bring him home, ending Hebert's day. Chad Kimsey took the ball for St. Louis and gave up a bunt single to Eric McNair that brought Miller home, making the score 6–3 in favor of Philadelphia. Grove retired the Browns in order in the top of the ninth to earn the victory, his twelfth in a row. His record was now an impressive 21–2, and baseball fans across the nation were beginning to take notice.

The third game against the Browns saw Roy Mahaffey take on Lefty Stewart in a fine pitchers' duel. Al Simmons doubled in the bottom of the second and scored when Bing Miller grounded into a double play. In the bottom of the fourth, Jimmy Moore, playing in center for the injured Haas, reached base on an error. Mickey Cochrane then singled to center. Al Simmons flied out, bringing Jimmie Foxx to the plate. Foxx drove one out of the park, and the A's led, 4–0. It was the twentieth home run of the season thus far for the Philadelphia cleanup hitter. That was it for the Athletics' scoring, as Stewart scattered three more hits the rest of the way. In the meantime, Mahaffey had been throwing a gem of a game, allowing only two hits through eight innings of work. In the top of the ninth, he walked Ski Melillo to lead off the inning before surrendering singles to Goose Goslin and Red Kress. Melillo scored on the Kress hit, making the score 4–1, and Connie Mack had seen enough. Rube Walberg was sent in to relieve Mahaffey. Walberg got the first two Browns batters he faced to ground out, but Goslin was able to score on a fielder's choice. St. Louis sent Earl McNeely to the plate to pinch-hit with two outs, but Walberg got him to fly out to left to end the game and preserve the 4–2 victory.

Lefty Grove and the 1931 Philadelphia Athletics

The final game of the series on July 30 matched Waite Hoyt against Sam Gray. The A's got to Gray early and often, scoring two in the first inning and chasing the St. Louis starter with two more in the second. Dick Coffman came in to relieve Gray in the third and had no better luck retiring A's hitters. Mickey Cochrane stung Coffman for a two-run homer in the bottom of the fourth and nailed him for a solo shot in the sixth. Philadelphia led the contest, 8–0, going into the seventh. Hoyt had given up only three hits thus far and seemed completely in control. He started to run out of gas a little in the seventh, however, when a lead-off double was followed by a home run by Lin Sorti. Another two-run shot, swatted by Goose Goslin in the top of the eighth, cut the Philadelphia lead in half and started to make things interesting. Mack decided to stay with his veteran hurler, though, and sent Hoyt back out in the top of the ninth to finish what he had started. Hoyt got the first two outs of the inning before surrendering another run, then got Melillo to fly out to center to end the game. The A's won, 8–5, and Hoyt improved his record to 8–9, recording his fifth win in six decisions since coming to Philadelphia. Mack was looking like a genius in bringing the veteran on board as a complement to his staff. The change of scenery between Detroit and Philadelphia had made a huge difference for Hoyt, who pitched like he had in his heyday.

The team opened the month of August with a series in Washington against the Senators. Rube Walberg was on the hill, opposed by Firpo Marberry, in what promised to be a great pitching matchup. The game did not fail to live up to its billing. Walberg gave up only two runs in his complete-game effort, but Marberry bested him by allowing only a single score. Doc Cramer had a big day filling in for Mule Haas, going four-for-five with a run scored. The problem was that the rest of the A's team managed only three more hits to go along with Cramer's big day. The Washington win allowed the Senators to gain ground on the A's, but Connie Mack was not terribly worried. His club still held a comfortable eleven-game cushion over Walter Johnson's team, and there was no reason to think that the red-hot A's would cool down enough for Washington to mount a serious challenge for the pennant.

Game two featured Hank McDonald against Sam Jones. McDonald had been throwing great ball lately, and when Philadelphia put up four

Six. *Dog Days and Another Winning Streak*

runs in its first at-bat, it seemed as if he would have easy sailing for the rest of the game. Jones had been chased without recording an out, and General Crowder took over for the Senators on the mound. McDonald returned the favor, however, when he was also sent to an early shower in the first inning after retiring only one Washington hitter and being tagged for four runs. Waite Hoyt came in to relieve McDonald and finished the inning to move to the top of the second. Crowder blanked Philadelphia in their half of the frame, then the Washington bats got to Hoyt for four more runs in their at-bat. The Senators led, 8–4, and Crowder settled in to keep Philadelphia from mounting any serious threats for the remainder of the game. Eddie Rommel started the third, in relief of Hoyt, and allowed two more Washington scores in his six innings of work to give the Senators a 10–6 victory.

Washington went for a third straight win over Philadelphia, attempting to pull within single digits of the league leader, on August 3 in the first game of a doubleheader at Shibe Park. Lefty Grove took the mound in front of a large crowd to oppose Sam Jones. Most of the fans in the stands had come to see Grove attempt to win his thirteenth game in a row. Baseball enthusiasts all over the country were now taking note of each of Lefty's starts as he made his assault on the league record. Grove was spotted to a 3–0 lead in the bottom of the third inning when Cochrane, Simmons and Miller came through with RBI hits, and he made the advantage stand up. Working in and out of trouble throughout the game, Grove allowed eleven hits to the Washington batters, but gave up only two runs in the top of the eighth. He then closed the Senators out in the ninth to run his record to 22–2 and earn his lucky thirteenth consecutive victory.

Game two of the twin feature had George Earnshaw taking on Carl Fischer. The A's plated a run in the bottom of the second on an Al Simmons homer, but Washington came back with four in the top of the third. Philadelphia scratched out another run in its half of the third, then struck for three scores in the fourth, with the big blast being a two-run homer off the bat of Jimmie Foxx. Washington tied the score with a run in the sixth, but Phil Todt put the game away with a solo home run in the eighth to give the A's the 6–5 victory. The Senators had rapped out eleven hits in both games of the doubleheader but had dropped them both, falling to twelve games behind first-place Philadelphia.

The Athletics had two days off before opening the first game of a series with the Yankees in New York on August 6. Lefty Gomez faced off against Rube Walberg in this contest. Babe Ruth homered off Walberg in a four-run first that gave the Yankees an early lead. Gomez was tough on the A's, allowing only one run in eight innings of work. New York added an insurance run in the fifth, and the game went to the ninth with the Yankees leading, 5–1. Gomez got into some trouble in the last at-bat for Philadelphia, giving up two runs without recording an out. New York manager Joe McCarthy turned to Hank Johnson to put out the fire. Johnson did his job, but not without a bit of dramatics, giving up a hit and a walk before getting the third out. Philadelphia fell to their hated rivals, 5–3, as New York heated up and tried to pass Washington to take control of second place in the league.

Game two of the series on August 8 pitted George Earnshaw against the New York veteran ace, Red Ruffing. Both pitchers threw exceptional games, allowing a combined total of only nine hits and giving up but a single earned run apiece through nine innings. Errors in the field allowed each team to score unearned runs, which would be the difference in the game. New York plated two runs due to mishandled plays by Philadelphia fielders, while the A's received only one score as a result of a booted ball by the Yankees. In the end, Earnshaw took the loss in a 3–2 heartbreaker. The Yankees had been playing great ball lately, and the last two wins gave the New Yorkers hope that they could climb back into the race for the pennant in the final weeks of the season. With thirty-two wins in the last forty-nine games on their schedule, the Yanks would improve on their third-place standing by the time the season came to a close, but they would not catch the red-hot A's.

In the final game of the series, Connie Mack sent Roy Mahaffey to the mound to face George Pipgras. The Yankees were looking for a sweep, but Mahaffey had something else in mind. He baffled the Yankees through six innings, allowing only two hits to the imposing lineup of Yankees batters. Al Simmons launched a two-run homer in the third to give Philadelphia the lead and singled to lead off the sixth, eventually being brought home on a double by Bing Miller. Mahaffey got into trou-

Six. Dog Days and Another Winning Streak

ble not of his own making when New York came to bat in the seventh. Lyn Lary reached base on an error by Jimmie Foxx, then Eric McNair booted one that allowed Bill Dickey to get aboard. Tony Lazerri walked to load the bases, and Earle Combs came to the plate to pinch-hit for the pitcher. Mack made a pitching change, bringing Rube Walberg in to face Combs. Walberg struck out Combs, then got Sam Byrd to fly out, with Lary scoring on the sacrifice. Joe Sewell singled to right, bringing Dickey home, and Mack decided it was time to make another pitching change. Grove got the nod, taking the hill to face Babe Ruth. The Babe ripped a single to right off Lefty that brought Lazerri in to score, but then Grove knuckled down to strike out Lou Gehrig, ending the inning. Lefty allowed only one hit over the next two innings to secure the 5–3 win and earn his fifth save of the season.

Fielding errors were continuing to make games more interesting than they needed to be for the A's. The truth is that Philadelphia rated very well in the league in terms of the number of errors committed by the team, but it seemed as if the opposition made the A's pay for every miscue they made by bringing runs across the plate. Over the course of the 1931 season, Philadelphia errors accounted for one hundred runs being scored by the opposition. Grove was hit hardest of all Athletics pitchers by unearned runs. Nearly twenty percent of the eighty-eight runs he surrendered during the 1931 season were of the unearned variety.

After a day off for travel, Mack's boys opened a series with the Tigers at Navin Field on August 11. It was Lefty Grove's turn in the rotation, and he made the start despite the fact that he had pitched two-plus innings in the last game in New York. Vic Sorrell took the mound for Detroit, and the A's jumped on him in the top of the first when Max Bishop led off with a single. Mickey Cochrane's double put runners on second and third. Al Simmons then brought them both home with a double before Sorrell could get out of the inning. Sorrell got into more trouble in the second, when Eric McNair led off with a home run. Dib Williams followed with a single, and was still there after Lefty Grove struck out. Max Bishop walked, then Doc Cramer singled to bring Williams home. That was it for Sorrell. Charlie Sullivan came in to relieve the starter with Mickey Cochrane at the plate. Cochrane greeted him with a single to right, driving in Bishop. Al Simmons hit into a fielder's choice that scored Cramer, but then got thrown out attempting to steal second to end the inning. Philadelphia had put four more on the board, and led the game, 6–0. Grove gave up a run on two hits in the bottom of the third, but that was all the offense Detroit would muster. In one of his best pitching efforts during the current winning streak, Grove scattered seven Tiger hits over nine innings while striking out six Detroit batters. In the eighth, he helped his own cause by leading off the inning with a single to right. Max Bishop and Doc Cramer followed with singles of their own, and Grove came in to score one of his few runs of the season. Cochrane then lifted a fly ball to left that brought Bishop home for an 8–1 lead. Grove made it stand up to extend his streak to fourteen games and up his record to 23–2.

Two more wins were needed to tie the record and three to take sole ownership of it. This was not the first time that Lefty had been within striking distance of the American League consecutive wins record. During the 1928 season, Grove strung together fourteen straight wins before going to New York to face the Yankees. At the end of seven innings, the A's held a 3–1 lead over the Murderer's Row lineup, and Lefty only had to get six more outs to extend his streak. But things started to fall apart in the eighth when he walked Earle Combs. Mark Koenig followed with an infield hit, and Combs advanced to third on a wild throw by Jimmy Dykes. Lou Gehrig was at the plate, and Grove muscled up to throw one past the Iron Man, but he ended up throwing it away on a wild pitch that allowed Combs to score. Gehrig then ducked out of the way to evade an inside pitch from Lefty, but the ball hit his bat, ending up in short left field with a bloop single that scored Koenig. Babe Ruth came to the plate with the game tied at three, and it was power against power. Grove reared back and threw heat at the Babe, getting a ball and a strike in his first two pitches. On pitch number three to Ruth, Lefty threw a blazing fastball, challenging the Sultan of Swat to beat him with his best. Ruth got all of it, driving the ball deep to right field for a two-run homer that gave the Yankees a 5–3 lead that would eventually become the final score.[3]

But this was another year. Lefty was not only pitching better this year than he had in 1928, he was also experiencing a better run of luck.

Six. Dog Days and Another Winning Streak

Everyone felt that if Grove was to break the record, this would be his season. One thing was sure: Lefty would practice the routine that had been a part of his baseball career since joining the Orioles in 1920. Tommy Thomas, who had been a teammate of Grove's in Baltimore, said that he "went to sleep when it got dark and got up when it got light. He didn't socialize much. Well, he was from a small town. He was close to his family and he was honest and industrious." In 1921, Lefty had married his childhood sweetheart, Ethel Gardner, and the couple would have two children, Robert and Doris. Lefty rented a house for his family in his team's home city during the baseball season. In the offseason, the family returned to Lonaconing, where Grove had bought a house. The day before a start usually witnessed a steak dinner followed by a cigar or two. A little extra sleep on game day was followed by a late breakfast or early lunch and a leisurely trip to the park to face the day's opponents.

The next day the two teams got together for a game where the offense ruled. George Earnshaw faced Art Herring in a game that featured twenty-seven hits and forty total base runners in twelve innings of play. The A's jumped on Herring for four runs in the first two innings and held a 6-4 lead going into the bottom of the seventh. But the Tigers plated two in their at-bat, pulling even on the scoreboard. Detroit brought their third pitcher, George Uhle, into the game in the seventh inning, and he did not allow the A's to score another run in six innings of work. Earnshaw went the full twelve innings of the game, giving up a score in the bottom of the twelfth and taking the 7-6 loss in heartbreaker fashion. The game should have ended in regulation with a victory for Earnshaw, but Philadelphia errors led to two unearned runs that kept Detroit in the game and allowed the Tigers to win.

Rube Walberg started for the A's in the last contest of the three-game set in Detroit. Earl Whitehill was his mound opponent, as the Tigers looked to take the rubber game of the series. Al Simmons hit a solo home run and scored twice as the A's built a 5-0 lead through the fifth inning. Walberg pitched a gem, allowing only four hits in a complete-game effort, but he did give up six walks against only three strikeouts. Detroit squeezed two runs out of their plate opportunities but fell short in a 5-2 loss, as Philadelphia improved its record to 79-31, flirting with fifty games over .500.

Lefty Grove and the 1931 Philadelphia Athletics

August 14 was a travel day, as the team made its way to Cleveland for a much-anticipated series with the Indians. The thing that made the series so important to the fans was the fact that Lefty Grove was scheduled to pitch in game one in a quest for his fifteenth straight win. The August 15 matchup featured Grove against Wes Ferrell, the Indians' ace. Grove was staked to an early cushion when the A's parlayed two hits, two walks and an error into three runs in the top of the first. Grove cruised through the first five innings but gave up two runs on three hits in the bottom of the sixth. The A's got one of the runs back in the top of the seventh, when Grove walked to keep the inning going, before Dib Williams came in to score on a Doc Cramer single. Lefty served up a leadoff home run to Earl Averill in the bottom of the eighth to make the score 4–3, but sat down the Indians in order in the bottom of the ninth to preserve the victory and run his streak to fifteen in a row. The baseball world was now intently watching Grove's assault on the record, as fans checked the calendar to see when his next start should take place. A win in that game would give him a piece of the record and tie him with Smoky Joe Wood and Walter Johnson.

Roy Mahaffey got the start in game two of the series against the Indians, opposing Sarge Connally. Philadelphia put up six runs in the game, showing off its power with home runs by Mickey Cochrane and Doc Cramer and a run-scoring double by Jimmie Foxx. But a great deal of the power for the team was not in the lineup. Mule Haas was still out, waiting for his fracture to heal, and he was now joined by Al Simmons. Simmons had always had trouble with weak ankles, and now he suffered from a sprained and infected left ankle that kept him out of the lineup. Simmons traveled to Milwaukee to seek treatment and would miss the next two weeks of the season. In the meantime, light-hitting Jimmy Moore replaced him in the lineup.[4] Mahaffey was the story of this day, however, as he held the Indians in check through seven innings but had to depart in the eighth after giving up two runs to make the score 6–4. Waite Hoyt came in to finish the eighth, and Rube Walberg took the mound in the ninth, sitting down the Indians in order to earn his third save and preserve the win for Mahaffey, who was now an impressive 13–2.

On August 19, the A's opened a series against the White Sox at

Six. Dog Days and Another Winning Streak

Comiskey Park. Baseball fans in Chicago were buzzing because Lefty Grove was schedule to get the start while making a bid for baseball history that night. The future Hall of Fame pitcher, forty-two-year-old Red Faber, got the nod from Sox manager Donie Bush to take the mound for Chicago. The Athletics posted two runs on the board in the top of the second, when Faber botched a play that allowed Bing Miller and Eric McNair to cross the plate. They added another in the third when McNair singled to right, driving in Jimmie Foxx, who had been hit by a pitch. McNair would later single to lead off the eighth inning, and would come around to score three batters later on a single by Doc Cramer. That was it for the Philadelphia scoring for the day, but it was more than enough run support for Lefty. Grove held the White Sox scoreless through eight innings, scattering five hits while striking out five and did not allow a walk. In the bottom of the ninth, Carl Reynolds led off for Chicago and singled to center. Lew Fonseca followed with a double that drove Reynolds in and plated the first run of the game for the White Sox. Bob Fothergill reached on an error by Max Bishop before Luke Appling came to the plate to pinch-hit for John Kerr. Grove got Appling on a dribbling grounder just in front of the catcher, and coaxed Bill Cissell to ground to the shortstop, which brought Fonseca home with an unearned run. Chicago's last hope, Frank Grube, came to the plate representing the tying run, but Grove got him to ground out to the shortstop to end the game. Lefty had just earned a piece of history. He had won his sixteenth consecutive game, ensuring that his name would be mentioned every time the American League consecutive winning streak was discussed. One more victory and he could take sole possession of the all-time record. His record for this season improved to an incredible 25–2, and he was leading the league by a large margin with his 2.02 ERA. Indeed, Lefty was adding to his already-established reputation of being the best pitcher currently in the game, and providing ammunition for those who argued that he was the best of all-time.

Waite Hoyt got the start against Tommy Thomas in game two of the series. Neither pitcher had a winning record, and the batters on both sides hoped for a productive day. The White Sox broke into the lead when Lew Fonseca drove in a run in the bottom of the first. The A's pulled even in the top of the second when Bing Miller scored on an error by Sox first baseman Lu Blue. Hoyt gave up another run in the fourth on a walk and two hits, but Philadelphia plated two in the top of the fifth on two walks and two hits to take a 3–2 lead. Things got ugly for Hoyt in the bottom of the inning, as Billy Sullivan lead off with a triple to right. Carl Reynolds rapped a single that drove in Sullivan, then advanced to third on a single by Lew Fonseca. Bob Fothergill hit a ball to shortstop, but Dib Williams bobbled it, allowing Fothergill to reach and Reynolds to score. John Kerr reached on a fielder's choice bunt, and the bases were loaded with nobody out. Luke Appling then got everybody running with a single that brought home Fonseca and Fothergill. Bennie Tate singled to drive in Kerr and Appling, and the White Sox were still in business with six runs in and nobody out. Hoyt was able to get the next three batters to close the inning, but Chicago had batted around and taken an imposing 8–3 lead.

Eric McNair led off the top of the sixth with a single and advanced to second on an error by Sullivan. Dib Williams brought him home with a single to center, and crossed the plate when Hoyt swatted a double to left. When Max Bishop clouted a double to right, Hoyt scored the third A's run of the frame. Donie Bush had seen enough. Thomas got the hook, replaced on the mound by Vic Frazier, as the heart of the Philadelphia order came to the plate. Frazier hit Doc Cramer with a pitch, then walked Mickey Cochrane to load the bases with nobody out. Jimmy Moore and Jimmie Foxx both struck out, and Bing Miller grounded to second to end the threat and get Frazier out of the inning. Hoyt surrendered another run in the sixth, and two more in the seventh before Eddie Rommel came in to the game to replace him. Frazier did not allow another run in his four innings of relief, and the Athletics fell, 11–6.

Rube Walberg started the third game of the four-game series against Bob Weiland on August 21. The contest proved to be a slugfest with twenty-seven total runs scored. The A's took an early lead in the first when Max Bishop led off with a single, and eventually scored on a wild pitch by Weiland. The White Sox tied the score when they got to Walberg for three straight hits to lead off the second. Philadelphia recaptured the lead by scoring two unearned runs in the top of the third, but gave it back in the fourth when Walberg got a little wild, allowing two walks and a hit before Lu Blue doubled to left, clearing the bases. Trailing, 4–

Six. Dog Days and Another Winning Streak

3, the A's came to the plate in the top of the fifth. Weiland got Walberg to ground out to short, then gave up a walk to Bishop, a single to Cramer, and a walk to Cochrane to load the bases. When Weiland hit Jimmy Moore with a pitch to bring Bishop in to score, he earned an early exit from the game. Pat Caraway came in to replace him, and promptly walked Jimmie Foxx to force in another run. Bing Miller tripled to clear the bases, and Caraway joined Weiland in the showers, as Jim Moore came in to pitch. Moore got the final two outs, but the A's had taken an 8–4 lead.

Philadelphia tacked on two more in the sixth when Doc Cramer homered with Max Bishop aboard. With a 10–4 lead, the game seemed just about over, but Chicago had other ideas. Walberg gave up four runs in the sixth, and was responsible for the runner on second when Roy Mahaffey came in to replace him. Mahaffey retired the first man he faced, then gave up a double to Billy Sullivan that closed the book on Walberg. The A's posted three in the top of the seventh on a three-run blast by Dib Williams, but Chicago kept the pressure on with three in the bottom of the frame. Grant Bowler came into the game to pitch for Chicago, and though he closed out the seventh, he was touched up for two more A's runs in the eighth. No runs were scored in the ninth, the only inning of the game that did not see a tally posted to the scoreboard, and the A's escaped with a 15–12 win in a scoring outburst that must have thrilled all fans in the stands who favored offense over pitching.

The following day, Rube Walberg once again was announced as the starting pitcher despite the fact that he had worked 5⅓ innings the previous day. Pat Caraway, who had also pitched the previous day, was announced for the White Sox. Caraway had only faced two batters, and would be much fresher than Walberg. Instead of being fatigued, Walberg seemed pumped up on this day, as he kept the White Sox batters off stride, scattering seven hits and allowing only one unearned run in the seventh in a complete-game effort. Philadelphia scored early and often against three Chicago pitchers, including Bob Weiland, the starter from the day before. Jimmie Foxx hit his twenty-second home run of the year, while Jimmy Moore temporarily assumed not only Al Simmons' place in the lineup but also his presence, going three-for-five with a double, a home run, and three RBIs. The 7–1 final was a great win for both Walberg and the team, but few people were taking time to savor the victory. Connie Mack had announced that Lefty Grove would get the start in the first game of a doubleheader against the Browns in St. Louis the following day. All eyes focused on St. Louis for what promised to be a record-breaking day in this memorable season.

In an odd move, St. Louis manager Bill Kellifer asked for a volunteer from among his pitching staff to face Grove, and Dick Coffman stepped forward to accept the challenge. Coffman was only 5–9 on the season, and hardly seemed to be a worthy opponent for Grove. The Browns were 50–68 and trailed Philadelphia by 34½ games in the standings. On paper, it seemed like an automatic victory for Lefty, probably even a laugher, but the game is not played on paper. The A's were not exactly the same team that had been piling up victories all summer. Haas and Simmons were both still out of the lineup, and shortstop Joe Boley and third baseman Jimmy Dykes would miss this game with cramps. Grove was on top of his game, scattering seven hits and giving up only one run on an RBI double to Ski Melillo in the bottom of the third. On most any other day, that would be good enough to win, especially with the potent lineup the A's could send to the plate. But Coffman was equal to the challenge, and he shut the Philadelphia batters down in possibly the best performance of his career. A's batters were limited to three total hits by Coffman, who pitched a nine-inning shutout.

The controversy in the game came as a result of the run-scoring double by Melillo. The ball was hit to left field, a line drive right at Jimmy Moore. As he looked into the sun, the substitute left fielder misjudged the ball initially, and came in on it. Realizing the ball was carrying better than he had anticipated, Moore frantically tried to get back. He stretched out his arm as the ball descended, but it glanced off the end of the fingertips of his glove and fell to earth. Lefty glared out to left field and slapped his glove off his leg, as the redness of his face displayed to all the exasperation he felt. At the end of the inning, Grove entered the dugout and shot a daggered stare to Moore before seating himself to hopefully watch his teammates get that run back.[5]

For his part, Moore assumed all responsibility for the ball not being caught. Not one to take the easy out of complaining about the sun in his eyes, Moore stated, "If I'd stood still, I'd have caught it. If I'd been

Six. Dog Days and Another Winning Streak

sitting on a chair, I'd have caught it. But Melillo was a light hitter and I moved in two steps. The ball was hit harder'n I thought, and it just nipped off the end of my glove." Moore may have taken total responsibility for not making the play, but the person Grove was furious with was Al Simmons. Lefty felt that Simmons was well enough to have been in the lineup, and reasoned that he would have easily made the routine play, preventing the run from scoring. In all fairness, Simmons had volunteered to make the start, but Connie Mack told him to take some more time off to allow his ankle to heal completely. At the end of the game, when Lefty hit the clubhouse, he ripped off his shirt and began throwing anything he could get his hands on. A rubble of broken chairs and dented lockers was the result of his tirade, as teammates tried to simply stay out of his way and out of the line of fire. Connie Mack approached his star later at the hotel in an effort to calm him down. "Robert," Connie reasoned, "that boy pitched a great game, and if we had played them all night we still probably wouldn't have scored." Mack kept arguing the point until Grove finally admitted that he had thrown a fine game.[6] To be sure, the Philadelphia lineup that day contributed to Coffman's fine performance, but some things are just meant to be. Lefty lost his bid to break the consecutive wins record in a 1–0 decision in the only shutout suffered by the Athletics during the entire 1931 season. The streak was now over, however, and it remained for the A's to close out the regular season on a good note and get ready to face the National League representative in the World Series, where they would surely continue another streak by winning their third consecutive title.

SEVEN
The Drive to a Third Pennant

There were only thirty-five games remaining in the season as the teams took the field to play the second game of the twinbill in St. Louis. Waite Hoyt squared off against Lefty Stewart in the nightcap, which featured the A's offensive power to the extreme. Philadelphia rapped out seventeen hits, five of them doubles, en route to a 10–0 drubbing of the Browns. Grove must have wondered where all that offense was in game one of the doubleheader. Maybe it was just a bad day for any pitcher nicknamed Lefty. Lefty Stewart received no run support from the Browns, who managed only four hits against Hoyt in his complete-game shutout performance. Grove had watched the second game from the dugout, still seething over his loss, and probably contemplating how the team could score so often for Hoyt when they could not manage a single run for him.[1] Many years later, the loss of that game would still haunt him, and until the day he died, Lefty held Al Simmons responsible for his streak ending short of breaking the record.

Roy Mahaffey started the third game of the series on August 23. Mahaffey was quietly putting together a modest streak of his own, having not lost a game since July 9. He had won seven straight in that six-week period, and entered the game with an impressive 13–2 record. Mahaffey faced Sam Gray as his mound opponent. All of the scoring that mattered took place in the first inning, as five of the first six batters Gray faced got hits to stake Mahaffey to a 4–0 lead. Goose Goslin homered in the bottom of the inning to account for the only St. Louis run of the contest. The A's got an insurance run in the top of the ninth when Jimmy Dykes doubled, and was brought in by a Dib Williams single. Mahaffey scattered five hits and gave up only two walks in earning the 5–1 victory and running his record to 14–2. Though he was not considered to be the

Seven. The Drive to a Third Pennant

best pitcher on the staff or even one of the big three that Connie Mack relied on, Mahaffey was hot, and his successful spot starts were a big reason the A's continued to dominate in the race for the pennant.

Eddie Rommel got a rare start in the fourth game of the series with the Browns on August 25. George Blaeholder was scheduled to pitch for St. Louis. The Browns took a lead in the bottom of the first when Rommel walked the leadoff batter, Fred Schulte. After retiring the next hitter, Rommel faced Goose Goslin, who tripled to bring in Schulte. That was all that Rommel would surrender this day. The Browns managed five more hits over the next eight innings, but they were not able to push another man across the plate. In the meantime, Philadelphia plated two in the third to take the lead for good. They added single runs in the fourth and ninth to make the game a 4–1 final. Thus far, St. Louis had been able to scratch out only three runs in four games against the A's. In the meantime, Philadelphia had pushed nineteen runs across the plate, and Lefty Grove must have scratched his head wondering how he could have lost the only game of the series amid such numbers.

Rube Walberg got the start against Lefty Stewart in the final game of the extended series in St. Louis. The Browns finally brought their bats with them on this day, nailing Walberg for fourteen hits and nine runs in 7⅓ innings of work. It wasn't quite as bad as the box score indicated for Walberg, as only six of the runs were earned. An error by Dib Williams led to three unearned scores, as Philadelphia miscues continued to result in opposing runs. The Athletics ended up with nine hits of their own, four of them doubles, but they could only manage five runs and fell, 9–5, in the contest. St. Louis had won a moral victory in the series. Not only had they taken two of the five games played against the best team in baseball, but they had been responsible for ending the winning streak of the great Lefty Grove.

August 27 was a travel day, as the A's returned to Philadelphia to open a homestand against their archrivals, the Yankees. Roy Mahaffey was given the ball in the opener on August 28, opposing Red Ruffing. Connie Mack must have been dejected as he scanned the bleachers at Shibe Park to see the small crowd of 13,000 that showed up to see his first-place club take on the mighty New Yorkers. Mahaffey pitched another strong game, but he trailed New York, 4–2, as his team went to the bat rack in the bottom of the seventh. Bing Miller led off with a walk, and four singles later the A's had taken a 5–4 lead in the game and gotten Mahaffey off the hook. George Earnshaw came in to pitch the final two innings, shutting out the Yankees to earn his fifth save on the season. Mahaffey won his ninth consecutive game, though no one in the baseball world speculated that he had a chance to challenge for the league record that Grove had so narrowly missed.

Game two of the series was a matchup of Leftys. Lefty Grove would take on Lefty Gomez, as both teams ran their aces to the mound. Gomez lasted only two innings, as the A's chased him in the top of the third before he could record an out. Lefty Grove started the inning with a walk, and Max Bishop followed him with another free pass. Doc Cramer reached base on an error by Lyn Lary that allowed Grove to score. Mickey Cochrane singled, bringing in Bishop, and Jimmy Moore walked to load the bases. Jimmie Foxx brought them all home with a triple to center, and Gomez was on his way to an early shower. Ivy Andrews came in to record the three outs to get New York out of the inning without any further damage. Grove held the Yanks scoreless on two hits through five innings of work. The A's added to their lead in the bottom of the fifth when Jimmie Foxx belted his twenty-third home run of the season with Mickey Cochrane aboard. Grove got the first batter he faced in the top of the sixth to pop out, then gave up a double to Sam Byrd. Joe Sewell followed with a single, and Babe Ruth was walked to load the bases. A grand slam home run to Lou Gehrig chased Lefty from the game, and Rube Walberg came in to replace him. Walberg allowed no hits in his 3⅔ innings of work, and Philadelphia walked away with the 7–4 win.

August 30 found the Athletics in Washington ready to take on the Senators. Eddie Rommel's good work in his last outing against the Browns earned him another start against General Crowder. Washington got three runs in the first two innings and posted Crowder to a lead he would never relinquish. Rommel drove in Jimmy Dykes for the only Philadelphia run in the fifth inning, and the A's went on to lose the game, 5–1. Washington was still in second place, but at 15½ games behind in the standings with twenty eight games to go in the season, Athletics fans were already starting the countdown for clinching the pennant. Connie Mack and his boys did not have time to contemplate such matters. After

SEVEN. *The Drive to a Third Pennant*

the game they had to catch a train for the trip back to Philadelphia, where they would open a series with Boston the next day.

Waite Hoyt was pitted against Wilcy Moore in a great pitching matchup that brought the month of August to a close. Neither pitcher surrendered a run through the first six innings. In the bottom of the seventh, Hoyt walked and advanced to third on a double by Max Bishop. Doc Cramer's single to left brought Hoyt and Bishop both in to score, and gave the A's a 2–0 lead. Jimmie Foxx hit his twenty-fourth home run of the season in the eighth to pad the lead, and Hoyt sat down the opposing hitters in order in the ninth to earn the 3–0 victory and improve his record to a single game under .500, at 9–10. Hoyt was 6–2 since joining the A's, and his contributions, along with those of Mahaffey, amounted to a combined record of 21–4, not bad for a starter who was number four on the depth chart and a mid-season pickup.

The team started the month of September by opening a two-game set with the Senators at Shibe Park. Rube Walberg got the start against Sam Jones. Jones gave up ten hits and three walks in nine innings, but the A's were able to score only one run in the bottom of the fifth. Walberg gave up thirteen hits along with four walks in surrendering five runs. The 5–1 loss dropped Walberg's record to 19–9.

Roy Mahaffey brought his nine-game winning streak to Shibe Park on September 2 to face General Crowder. The Senators opened the scoring in the second by plating a run on a walk and two hits. Ossie Bluege homered in the fourth, the Senators scratched out two more runs in the fifth, and Heinie Manush capped the Washington scoring with a home run in the seventh. Crowder kept the A's scoreless through eight innings before getting into a little trouble in the bottom of the ninth. George Earnshaw pitched the top of the ninth in relief of Mahaffey, and he led off the bottom of the frame with a single to center. Phil Todt was put in the game to run for Earnshaw. Bishop and Cramer made outs, bringing Mickey Cochrane to the plate. Cochrane doubled to right, bringing home Todt, and scampered home on a single by Jimmy Moore. But that was the end of the rally. Crowder got Jimmie Foxx to bounce into a force play that ended the inning and gave Washington the 5–2 win. The Senators had accomplished an uncommon feat in 1931 by beating the A's in back-to-back games.

Lefty Grove and the 1931 Philadelphia Athletics

September 3 was an off-day as the team traveled to Boston for a five-game set with the Red Sox. Mack turned to Lefty Grove to stop the short two-game slide, and the ace did not disappoint. In classic Grove form, he gave up only three hits while striking out seven to shut out the Red Sox in a complete-game performance. Ed Durham got the start for Boston and pitched an excellent game, as well. Philadelphia was able to scratch out only six hits, but one was Jimmie Foxx's twenty-fifth home run, with Jimmy Moore aboard. The big blast came in the top of the seventh and was the only scoring either team could muster for the game. Grove allowed only one hit in the last three Boston at-bats but erased that runner in a double play and earned his twenty-seventh win of the season.

Waite Hoyt started the second game of the series against Jack Russell. Boston's scoring woes continued, as Hoyt allowed only a single run on seven hits in his complete-game outing. Philadelphia jumped on Russell for three runs in the first and two more in the second to take a lead Hoyt would never give up. An A's run in the top of the fifth gave Hoyt a 5–0 advantage before Boston scratched out its single tally in the bottom of the frame. Hoyt cruised to the 5–1 victory, which evened his record at 11–11 on the season. Philadelphia was now a whopping fifty-five games over .500, and the A's magic number had been reduced to nine games.

The third game of the series featured George Earnshaw in a match-up against Danny MacFayden in the first game of a doubleheader. Doc Cramer got things going for the A's in the top of the first by knocking a single to center. MacFayden then hit Mickey Cochrane with a pitch before giving up an RBI single to Jimmie Foxx. MacFayden then kept things close by blanking Philadelphia for the next four innings. The A's broke the game open in the sixth, when Mickey Cochrane and Jimmy Moore opened with singles. Foxx followed with a ground ball to short that erased Moore on a force play, leaving runners on first and third. Bing Miller singled to score Cochrane, and Phil Todt walked to load the bases. Dib Williams hit a sacrifice fly that brought Foxx home, and Earnshaw helped his own cause with a single to center that plated Miller. MacFayden was chased, and Boston turned to its bullpen in the top of the seventh. Philadelphia scored runs in each of the final three innings, however, and went to the bottom of the ninth leading, 8–0. In the mean-

Seven. The Drive to a Third Pennant

time, Earnshaw had been pitching one of the best games of his career. Allowing no walks through nine innings, he was posting a no-hitter through seven. Boston second baseman Marty McManus led off the eighth with an infield single that spoiled Earnshaw's no-hit bid. That was the only hit the Red Sox were able to muster in the game, however, as Earnshaw sat down the rest of the Boston hitters in order, nailing down a one-hit shutout for his eighteenth win of the season.

Rube Walberg started the second game of the twinbill scheduled for September 5, hoping to get back on the winning track. Walberg had lost his last two decisions, and his record resided close to .500 since the last week in June. He would be opposed in this game by Wilcy Moore, whose ERA was respectable at under four runs per game despite the fact that he had a losing record. The Red Sox jumped on Walberg for two runs in the bottom of the first inning, but Philadelphia surged back to take the lead with one in the fourth and two in the fifth. Boston answered with three in the sixth and added an insurance run in the seventh to take a 6–3 lead that would stand up as the final score. It was a hard-luck loss for Walberg, who pitched all nine innings, as two Philadelphia errors had once more led to the opposition pushing runs across the plate. Only three of the Red Sox scores had been earned, and Walberg deserved a better fate, as the loss dropped his record to 19–10.

Eddie Rommel took the ball in the final game of the series against Milt Gaston. Rommel worked hard throughout the game, trying to limit any damage caused by the ten Boston hits he surrendered. To his credit, he did not issue a free pass in nine innings of work, and made the Boston batters hit the ball to get on base. The Red Sox were able to cluster their hits for two runs in the third and one in the eighth. Gaston gave up eight hits for five runs with the big blasts being home runs off the bats of Mickey Cochrane and Dib Williams. Eddie Rommel helped his own cause by going two-for-four and scoring two runs. Philadelphia closed out the five-game set in Boston with a 5–3 win and shaved another game off its magic number.

September 6 was a travel day as the A's returned home to Philadelphia to prepare for a two-game series against the Yankees. A doubleheader, the second in three days, featured Roy Mahaffey going against Ivy Andrews in the opener. Mahaffey had faced the Yankees on August

28, and had pitched a strong game against the New Yorkers to earn the victory. The Yankees were ready for him this day, though, and he would not get out of the first inning. Earle Combs led off the game with a walk, then promptly stole second. A Joe Sewell single brought him home for a quick New York lead. Babe Ruth followed with a walk, and a wild pitch by Mahaffey allowed the runners to advance to second and third. A single to right by Lou Gehrig scored another run, and when Mahaffey walked Ben Chapman to load the bases, Connie Mack had seen enough. Hank McDonald came in to relieve Mahaffey with no one out. McDonald issued a base on balls to Lyn Lary that drove in Babe Ruth, then Bill Dickey hit a ball to shortstop that Dib Williams misplayed, allowing another run to score. Unable to find the plate, McDonald then walked Tony Lazzeri and Ivy Andrews to plate two more runs before joining Mahaffey with a quick exit. Jim Peterson came into the game as the third A's pitcher of the inning. Peterson walked both men he faced to drive in two more runs before Mack gave him the hook and sent Eddie Rommel to the mound. Rommel struck out Babe Ruth, Lou Gehrig and Ben Chapman to finally end the nightmare and get Philadelphia off the field. The Yankees had sent fourteen men to the plate and scored eight runs on only two hits. They had benefited greatly from a Philadelphia error and eight free passes. Rommel remained in the game in a mop-up role as Connie Mack conceded this game had gotten away from his team. Rommel allowed seven more runs in nine innings of work as the Yankees won a 15–3 laugher to open the series.

Things got little better for the A's in the nightcap, when Waite Hoyt faced Gordon Rhodes. The A's took a slim 1–0 lead in the bottom of the fourth when Cochrane, Foxx and Todt all singled to bring a run home. That lead was short-lived, however, as the Yankees got their bats going in the top of the sixth. Babe Ruth led off the inning with a home run, and Lou Gehrig made it back-to-back round-trippers when he launched one out of the yard. Hoyt got Lary to ground out, but then Bill Dickey took him deep for the third home run of the inning and a 3–1 lead for the Yankees. Philadelphia got one of the runs back in the bottom of the frame when Cochrane singled and came home on a triple by Foxx. But the Yankees kept the pedal to the metal, scoring single runs in the seventh and eighth and adding a four-spot in the ninth, punctuated by

SEVEN. *The Drive to a Third Pennant*

home runs by Ruth and Lary. New York cruised to another easy victory, beating the A's, 9–4, to sweep the doubleheader.

Relieved to have the red-hot Yankees out of town, Philadelphia opened a two-game series with the Washington Senators at Shibe Park on September 8. Lefty Grove took the mound to halt the A's two-game slide, and was opposed by Sam Jones. Jimmie Foxx got things going for the A's in the bottom of the second when he singled to center and was later brought around to score on a two-run homer by Dib Williams. The Senators got three of the seven hits they would manage off Grove in the top of the third, scoring a run and cutting the Philadelphia lead in half. Jones then matched Grove pitch for pitch as neither team was able to score through the middle innings. The A's then got to Jones for eight runs on six hits, an error and a walk in the bottom of the seventh. The big clouts of the inning were a single by Grove that drove in two and a three-run inside-the-park home run by Jimmie Foxx, his twenty-sixth of the year. Lefty blanked Washington through the final two innings to earn the 10–1 victory and improve his record to 28–3. With an ERA of 1.98, there was no more dominating pitcher in the game at that time.

Rube Walberg started the second game against Washington on September 9, opposed by General Crowder. Walberg's struggles continued as he pitched an excellent game this day, allowing only two Washington runs on eight hits but still failed to record a win. The A's were held to six hits, and the only run they could muster came in the form of Jimmie Foxx's twenty-seventh home run with no one aboard. Walberg's record dropped to 19–11 as he continued to face hard knocks in trying to get back into the win column. This game featured Al Simmons' return to the lineup, but the rust of two weeks away from the game was evident in the star's zero-for-four performance.

The St. Louis Browns came to town on September 10 to begin a three-game set with the Athletics. George Earnshaw faced Wally Hebert in the opener, and Earnshaw continued with the fine pitching that had marked his previous outing. His teammates staked him to a 4–0 lead when they jumped on Hebert in the bottom of the first, scoring four runs on six hits and chasing the starter before he could record the final out of the inning. Bob Cooney came in to replace Hebert and get Eric McNair to ground out to end the frame. That was all the run support

Earnshaw needed. A mistake to Goose Goslin in the top of the sixth resulted in a three-run homer, but that was all the runs the Browns would get. Philadelphia pushed home two more in the seventh, and Earnshaw did the rest to get the 6–3 win, his nineteenth of the season.

Lefty Grove started the second game of the series, the first of a doubleheader, against Sam Gray. Attendance was a paltry 15,000 despite the fact that the Philadelphia ace was on the mound. In the top of the first, Grove issued a walk and gave up two base hits, one of them good for an RBI, before getting Red Kress to pop up for the first out of the inning. A second run then scored on an error by Eric McNair before Lefty could get out of the inning. For a while, it looked as if Gray would make the lead stand up, as he allowed only two Philadelphia hits through the first four innings. In the bottom of the fifth, Dib Williams reached base on an error by Browns shortstop Jim Levey. Lefty Grove then brought him home with a double to right that cut the St. Louis lead in half. In the bottom of the sixth, Phil Todt got a two-out single to right. Jimmy Moore brought him home with a triple to center, then scored on an error by center fielder Fred Schulte. Philadelphia had the lead and Lefty never looked back. Shutting out the Browns in the final three innings, Lefty took the 3–2 decision and upped his win total to twenty-nine.

The nightcap and concluding game of the series with St. Louis featured Waite Hoyt against Dick Coffman. Coffman's last outing against Philadelphia had been the memorable three-hit shutout that had stopped Grove's winning streak at sixteen games. He seemed to have lost little of his edge in this second matchup against the A's. The Browns gave him an early lead when they plated four runs in the top of the first, ending Hoyt's work for the day. Philadelphia came back with two in its half of the inning, when McNair, Cramer and Todt all singled to go along with a walk to Moore. But that was all they could do against Coffman, who scattered six hits over the remaining eight innings and kept Philadelphia from getting on the board again. In the meantime, the Browns got to A's reliever Roy Mahaffey for six runs over six innings to post the 10–2 victory. Coffman had the A's number, and Grove must have been thankful that he had started the first game of the twinbill instead of the nightcap.

The Indians came to town on September 14 as Philadelphia continued to enjoy a lengthy homestand. There were only thirteen games

SEVEN. *The Drive to a Third Pennant*

left in the season, and second-place Washington was 13½ games behind in the standings. The A's had successfully wrapped up their third straight pennant, and the only race remaining in the American League was for the runner-up position. Walberg got the start against Willis Hudlin in the first game of a doubleheader, as Rube sought to break his four-game losing streak. He had pitched well in his last two starts, however, suffering hard-luck losses in both outings. On this day, luck had nothing to do with the outcome. Walberg was not on his game as the Indians got to him for fourteen hits, scoring six runs in the process. The A's were able to put only two runs on the scoreboard in falling, 6–2, to the Tribe. Walberg suffered his fifth consecutive loss, and his record dropped to 19–12.

Waite Hoyt took the ball in the nightcap and was opposed by Clint Brown for the Indians. Both pitchers had losing records and high earned run averages, and the game promised to be an offensive show. The A's took a 1–0 lead in the bottom of the first, but Cleveland came back with two in the fourth to go on top. In the bottom of the frame, Philadelphia put six on the board, powered by a three-run homer by Phil Todt. Jimmy Moore homered in the fifth to give Hoyt an 8–2 lead, and it looked as if the game had been decided. But the Indians kept chipping away. They scratched out a run in the seventh and added two more in the eighth, making that the last inning of work for Hoyt. Philadelphia plated an insurance run in the bottom of the eighth, and George Earnshaw came in to pitch the top of the ninth. Earnshaw made things interesting by giving up two runs before getting any outs, but he then bore down to induce a double play and then got the final Cleveland batter on a ground out to end the game, earning his sixth save of the year and giving Hoyt the 9–7 victory.

Eddie Rommel was given the nod in the third game of the series against Mel Harder. The issue was decided after the first inning of play, as the A's surged to a 3–0 lead after their first at-bat. By the end of the third, Philadelphia was leading, 7–1, and the rout was on. Rommel won his sixth victory of the year in a 14–3 blowout of the Indians that boasted eighteen Athletic hits, sixteen of them singles. The win lifted Philadelphia to just one shy of the one hundred-win mark, at an impressive fifty-six games over .500.

Lefty Grove and the 1931 Philadelphia Athletics

George Earnshaw started the final game of the series against Wes Ferrell. Earnshaw was going for his twentieth win of the season when the teams took the field on September 16. The Tribe got to Earnshaw with five singles and a walk in the top of the second, and by the time the final out was recorded, five Cleveland runs had crossed the plate. Connie Mack decided to stay with his starter, and it proved to be a wise move. Earnshaw gave up only one more hit in his final seven innings and kept the Indians from scoring another run. Meanwhile, the A's started a rally with four runs in the bottom of the fifth, and went to the sixth trailing by a single score. When Philadelphia came to bat in its half of the frame, Jimmy Dykes led off with a double to left. Dib Williams singled to right, putting runners on the corners. Earnshaw then tied the game with a sacrifice fly that brought Dykes home. Eric McNair then came to the plate and swatted a two-run homer to give the Mackmen a 7–5 lead. Earnshaw retired Cleveland in order in the eighth but got into trouble in the ninth. Johnny Hodapp led off the inning with a single, and Glenn Myatt reached on an error by Dib Williams. With nobody out, Bibb Falk pinch-hit for Ed Montague and represented the potential winning run at the plate. Earnshaw struck out Falk, then induced Wes Ferrell to ground into a game-ending double play to notch his twentieth win of the season and elevate the team to the century mark in victories.

On September 18, Lefty Grove went for a milestone of his own, as the Chicago White Sox came to town. Grove was seeking the first thirty-win season of his career when he took on Chicago's Red Faber in the pitching matchup at Shibe Park. Grove gave up two hits in the top of the first, one of them a solo homer to Billy Sullivan. Chicago got only three more hits in the rest of the game, as Lefty struck out six and walked only one. Philadelphia took the lead in the bottom of the third when Grove led off the inning with a single, and was later followed by doubles from Jimmy Moore and Al Simmons. They added another score on an RBI single by Simmons in the fifth on their way to the 3–1 victory. Grove would win 172 total games in a seven-year stretch of twenty-victory seasons. This was the fifth year of that seven-year run, and the 1931 campaign would be the only time in his career that Lefty Grove ascended to the lofty plateau of thirty wins. He was not finished, however, as he had five more games to pitch before calling it a season.

Seven. *The Drive to a Third Pennant*

Rube Walberg got the start against the White Sox in the second game of the series, the first of what must have seemed like an endless string of doubleheaders. Bob Welland went to the mound for Chicago, as Walberg sought to end his losing streak and join Earnshaw in the twenty-victory club. In a year filled with streaks, it would be the third consecutive game in which a Philadelphia pitcher sought to pick up a milestone victory. Mule Haas was finally back in the Philadelphia lineup, which must have served as a good omen for the entire team. It wasn't one of Walberg's best outings of the season, as he gave up ten hits and six walks in nine innings pitched, but he was able to work in and out of trouble, limiting the White Sox to just three runs scored and blanking them through six innings. The A's got their scoring started in the first when Al Simmons and Jimmie Foxx each hit solo home runs. In the fourth, Jimmy Dykes led off with a single, then scored when Walberg flexed his muscles and belted a triple to bring him around. Mickey Cochrane led off the fifth with a double, and Simmons promptly doubled him home. The A's got another run in the sixth, then put an exclamation point on the game with four in the eighth. Walberg led off the inning with a single. Eric McNair batted for Max Bishop and singled to left. Doc Cramer grounded out, moving the runners up in the process, and Mickey Cochrane came to the plate. Cochrane plated three with his seventeenth home run of the season, and Al Simmons followed with his twenty-first round-tripper. Walberg improved his record to 20–12, and with all their starters back in the lineup, the A's seemed to be firing on all cylinders.

Waite Hoyt took on Tommy Thomas in the nightcap, and the veteran exhibited the sort of stuff that had made him a Yankee ace through the 1920s. Hoyt got two outs before he gave up the only hit the White Sox would get in the top of the first. The problem was that the hit was a double by Smead Jolley with Johnny Watwood aboard. Hoyt had walked Watwood, who scored on the two-bagger to give Chicago the lead. That was the last run the White Sox would score in the game, as Hoyt scattered five more hits over the remaining eight innings. Thomas kept the A's off the scoreboard until the fifth inning, when Jimmy Dykes led off with a double, then scored on an RBI single by Hoyt. Dykes doubled in two runs in the sixth to give Philadelphia the lead, and Hoyt went on to the 3–1 win, evening his record at 13–13. He was now 10–5 since joining the A's, and had made a significant contribution to the pennant drive.

The Detroit Tigers came to town to open a three-game series with Philadelphia on September 21. Eddie Rommel got another start against Chief Hogsett in game one of yet another doubleheader. Rommel and his knuckleball frustrated the Tigers by allowing only two runs on eleven hits and three walks. One Tigers base runner was caught stealing, and Rommel stranded eleven more in a complete-game effort that must have had the Detroit hitters scratching their heads. The A's didn't set the world on fire with their offense either, but the big boys in the lineup came through to give Rommel enough run support to win. Al Simmons drove in two, including a solo home run for his twenty-second on the year. Jimmie Foxx belted his twenty-eighth homer, also a solo shot, and the A's took the 3–2 decision for their 104th victory of the campaign. That total tied the 1929 club for a franchise record in wins with a few more games left in the season. The team would have the opportunity to add extra emphasis to what had already been a special season.

Tommy Bridges and George Uhle prevented Philadelphia from setting a franchise record in the second game of the doubleheader by beating the A's, 6–5. Jim Peterson got the start for Philadelphia as Mack gave his workhorses a break. Peterson blanked the Tigers through five innings but gave up two in the top of the sixth. Detroit added two more in the top of the seventh and led, 4–0, going to the bottom of the frame. Bridges got into trouble in the A's half of the seventh, and the bases were loaded with substitute catcher Joe Palmisano due to come to the plate. Connie Mack decided it was time for a pinch-hitter. Jimmie Foxx had also received a break in this game, but the manager sent him to the bat rack to select some lumber and hit for Palmisano. Foxx delivered with a grand slam that tied the score and gave Peterson new life. But the Tigers scored single runs in the eighth and ninth to take a 6–4 lead. Philadelphia rallied in its last at-bat but fell short, scoring only a single run to take the 6–5 loss.

George Earnshaw started the game against the Tigers on September 22 with Art Herring as his mound opponent. Connie Mack must have been beside himself as he looked out across the empty seats at Shibe

Seven. *The Drive to a Third Pennant*

Park. Only about 2,000 fans had turned out to see their pennant-winning A's take on Detroit. The team had won its third straight pennant, Lefty Grove had set a personal record for victories and tied the American League consecutive wins mark, but the season was proving to be a huge disappointment to ownership in terms of gate revenue. Attendance was dramatically down from the previous year, which also had been down from the year before that. Great teams cost money, and the Athletics simply were not generating the sort of income to pay for all the stars they had in their lineup. Mack could only hope that full seats in the World Series would bring in enough cash to keep the team afloat and pay everyone's salaries. If not, some hard business decisions would have to be made.

Earnshaw was staked to a 4–0 lead after one inning as the red-hot Foxx belted a three-run homer to close out the scoring in that frame. They added another score in the third on a walk, two singles and a sacrifice fly. Detroit got back in the game with three in the top of the fourth, but Philadelphia got two of them back in its half of the inning. Earnshaw gave up another run in the sixth before handing the ball to Roy Mahaffey. Mahaffey had no trouble retiring the Tigers in the seventh and eighth, but allowed the game to get interesting when he gave up two runs in the ninth before sitting down the last Detroit batter. Philadelphia had broken its own single-season wins record, and Earnshaw improved to 21–7, good enough to be the ace on any other team in the league, but not on one that had Lefty Grove in the rotation.

After a day off, Boston came to town for a short two-game set that would conclude the regular season home schedule for the A's. On September 24, Lefty Grove got the start against Wilcy Moore. Otis Miller led off the Boston second with a triple and scored on a sacrifice fly to give the Red Sox a 1–0 lead. Philadelphia plated two in the third and added five more over the next three innings. After tacking on two in the bottom of the eighth, Philadelphia led, 9–1, going into the top of the ninth. Lefty had given up only three hits thus far and had not allowed a walk while striking out four Boston batters. Grove got the first hitter of the inning before Marv Olsen worked him for a walk. Olsen advanced on a fly out by George Stumpf, and scored when Bill Sweeney singled to center. Earl Webb hit a ball to Dib Williams that should have been the last out of the game, but Williams bobbled it, allowing Webb to reach. Otis Miller once more made the A's pay for an error by rapping a double that brought home Sweeney and Webb. Lefty got the next batter to fly out to end the game, giving the A's the 9–4 win. It had been a classic performance for Grove: a complete-game effort, yielding only two earned runs on five hits. With two games left in the regular season, Grove's record was 31–3 with an ERA of 1.92.

In the second game of the series, Connie Mack gave some of his starters the day off, as Max Bishop, Mickey Cochrane and Al Simmons were all out of the lineup. He even rested his starting rotation by giving Lew Krausse his first start of the season. Ed Durham pitched for the Red Sox, who were looking forward to the end of a disappointing campaign. Krausse showed that he was up to the task, limiting the Boston batters to four hits in a complete-game effort and allowing only one unearned run in the fourth inning on a passed ball by backup catcher Joe Palmisano. Krausse led off the fifth by being hit with a pitch, and four of the next five Philadelphia hitters followed with singles that plated three runs and gave the A's a 3–1 lead. Krausse was at bat to lead off the next inning and again got things started by reaching base with a walk. Eric McNair singled to center, but Krausse was thrown out trying to reach third. Mule Haas walked before Palmisano doubled to center, bringing McNair home. Philadelphia added three more runs in the eighth, two of them on a wild pitch by Boston reliever Hod Lisenbee. The 7–1 final ran Philadelphia's record to 107 wins as the A's headed to New York to play the final game of the regular season against the Yankees.

Connie Mack chose Lefty Grove to make the start against the Yanks. Mack intended to ride his workhorse ace through the championship series, and the game against New York would be a good tune-up for post-season play, even though Grove would be pitching on just two day's rest. New York had posted the best record in the American League over the last several weeks of the season and succeeded in passing Washington to claim second place. To be sure, they were still a distant 14½ games behind Philadelphia, and had been eliminated from the pennant race a couple weeks earlier, but this was still the A's versus the Yankees, and rivalry games pay little attention to win-loss records. Ruth, Gehrig,

Seven. *The Drive to a Third Pennant*

Dickey and company relished the idea of ending Philadelphia's regular season with a loss, especially if it meant beating Lefty Grove to accomplish it. Besides, there was always next year, and the Yankees wanted to make a statement that they would be ready to pick up where they left off in 1931 to challenge the Athletics for the pennant when the 1932 season began. All of the Yankees regular starters were in the lineup to face Grove. On this day, it seemed as if it were the Yankees who were getting ready for post-season play, however, as the New York bats got to Grove for five runs on eight hits through three innings of play. The big blow was a two-run homer by Lou Gehrig in the third that ended Lefty's work for the day, as Earnshaw came in to replace him in the fourth and get some work. New York continued the offensive barrage against Earnshaw, plating seven runs in his three innings of work. Rube Walberg came in to mop up in the seventh and surrendered another Yankee run in the eighth, making the score a lopsided 13–1. Philadelphia had trotted a thirty-game winner and two twenty-game winners to the mound to face the mighty Yankees, and New York had responded by rapping out twenty hits, seven of them for extra bases, in a punishing exhibition of power that showed Joe McCarthy's boys were not going to lay down for anyone, especially the A's. Grove took his fourth loss of the season to go along with his thirty-one wins as the team limped out of New York to return to Philadelphia in preparation for the series with the National League champions. It would prove to be a rematch of the 1930 World Series, with the St. Louis Cardinals as Philadelphia's opponents.

Eight
Facing the Cardinals Again

The St. Louis Cardinals have had many fine teams among the nineteen squads that have captured the National League pennant and appeared in the World Series. Many would argue that the 1931 team was possibly the best of them all. The level of talent on the 1931 team was unquestionable, and they dominated the rest of the National League that year, winning 101 games and running away with the pennant with a thirteen-game lead over the second-place New York Giants. The A's and Cardinals were virtually the same teams as the ones that had met in the Fall Classic the previous year. The Cardinals had added a new center fielder, John "Pepper" Martin, and the A's had bolstered their rotation by picking up Waite Hoyt. The well-liked and good-natured Charles "Gabby" Street was the manager of the Cardinals, serving in his second year in charge. He had taken over the direction of the club in 1930, and in his first season at the dugout helm had led the Redbirds to a World Series appearance against these same Philadelphia Athletics.[1] The A's were the odds-on favorite to beat the Cardinals and capture their record-setting third straight title, but in many ways St. Louis matched up favorably with the powerhouse Philadelphia club. Star talent was abundant on the Cardinals' roster, including such future Hall of Fame notables as first baseman Jim Bottomley, second baseman Frankie Frisch, outfielder Chick Hafey, and pitchers Burleigh Grimes and Jessie Haines. The rest of the team was filled with solid performers who were good in the clutch, as well as being grind-it-out, hustling players. Chick Hafey led the National League with his .349 batting average, which may have been well below the .390 mark Al Simmons captured the American League crown with but still made him an accomplished and dangerous hitter. Bill Hallahan tied for the National League high in wins for the 1931 cam-

EIGHT. Facing the Cardinals Again

paign with 19 victories, and led the league with 159 strikeouts. When compared with Lefty Grove's 31 wins and 175 strikeouts, both American League records that year, Hallahan would seem to come up on the short end of the stick, but he was still a dominant pitcher for the Cardinals and the leader of the staff. In fact, many baseball historians feel that the 1931 Cardinals was the best St. Louis team of all-time. High praise for a franchise boasting nineteen appearances in the Fall Classic and holding eleven World Series titles, second only to the mighty New York Yankees. But as the former editor of *Sport Magazine*, Ed Fitzgerald, put it, the 1931 Cardinals "ran away with the National League, it defeated a great Athletic team, it had just about everything you could want in a ball club. It was a businesslike team. When we think about that old gag about a game not being over until the last man is out, we recall the Cardinals of 1931 and some of the games they pulled gleefully out of the fire in the eighth or ninth inning with devastating rallies."[2] While the Athletics symbolized the greatness of an established powerhouse team, guided by the patriarchal wisdom of the venerable Connie Mack, the Cardinals epitomized an up-and-coming collection of stars, led by the likeable and enthusiastic while still-fledgling Gabby Street. The Cardinals were still smarting over their lack of success in the series the previous year, and were thankful to have a rematch against the team that had kept them from claiming the crown. Everything pointed to an exciting rematch between the two squads, but the smart money was still on Philadelphia to make history and capture its third straight title.

Connie Mack and Gabby Street approached the series with different strategies regarding their starting rotations and the employment of their pitching staffs. Mack decided to go with a three-man rotation. Lefty Grove would be his workhorse and bear the greatest portion of the pitching work, followed by his other fireballer, George Earnshaw. In a somewhat-surprising move, Mack selected Waite Hoyt to be his third starter. Mack's decision must have been predicated upon the fact that Rube Walberg, though a twenty-game winner, had struggled mightily in the final part of the season, and the skipper obviously felt that he was not in top form. Hoyt, on the other hand, had provided a shot in the arm for the team since his acquisition from Detroit, going 10–5 for the A's and winning some big games down the stretch. Roy Mahaffey's 15–

4 record and his lights-out performances in several games in the second half of the season evidently was not enough to overcome Hoyt's reputation as a veteran ace with the Yankees and earn him a spot in Mack's rotation. He and Walberg would provide the A's with strong relief pitching out of the bullpen should the need arise.

Gabby Street opted to go with a four-man rotation in the series. Bill Hallahan would serve as his team's ace, but he would not be expected to carry quite the load Mack was placing on Grove's shoulders. In fact, Hallahan would not even be named as the Game One starter. Paul Derringer, the club's eighteen-game winner, would get the nod for the opener, possibly because Street did not wish to waste Hallahan's outing against Mack's probable Game One starter, Lefty Grove. Burleigh Grimes would also see significant service in the series, as would a surprise selection, Syl Johnson. Johnson had a modest 11–9 record during the regular season, but he earned his spot in the rotation with an impressive 3.00 ERA, the lowest on the Cardinals' staff. On paper, it looked like a mismatch. Hallahan and Derringer had combined for thirty-seven victories in the regular season, six more than Grove had won by himself, and fifteen less than Grove and Earnshaw had combined to put in the win column. Figuring that Grove would probably bring his 2.06 ERA into as many as three starts if the series went seven games, and remembering that the A's averaged more than 5.6 runs per game, it is easy to understand why most baseball prognosticators felt Philadelphia would have an easy time defending its crown and setting the record for consecutive titles.

Game One of the series took place at Sportsman's Park in St. Louis in front of a crowd of more than 38,000 fans. Lefty Grove was indeed Mack's choice as his starter, facing Paul Derringer in what would be the biggest game thus far in the twenty-four-year-old's rookie season. Derringer struck out Max Bishop and Mule Haas, then got Mickey Cochrane to ground out to short to sit down the A's in order in the top of the first. Grove took the mound and struck out Cardinal leadoff hitter and third baseman Andy High. Right fielder Wally Roettger then singled to center and moved to third on a single by second baseman Frankie Frisch. When first baseman Jim Bottomley slapped a ground ball through the infield, Roettger came in to score the first run

EIGHT. Facing the Cardinals Again

of the game. Grove then struck out left fielder Chick Hafey, and with two outs, looked to minimize the damage by holding St. Louis to a single tally. Into the batter's box stepped another Cardinals rookie, John "Pepper" Martin. The twenty-seven-year-old rookie center fielder had been a spark plug for St. Louis that season, in the field and at the plate, where his .300 batting average was among the team leaders. Self-confident and enthusiastic, Martin was not over-awed by Grove's reputation. He promptly rapped a double to right that brought Frisch home. It was the first of several big hits Martin would have in a series that would serve as his coming-out party and make Pepper Martin a star in the baseball world. Lefty got catcher Jimmie Wilson to ground out to short to end the inning and get the A's off the field. St. Louis had given Grove a harsh welcome, touching up the ace pitcher for four hits and two runs in its first at-bat. But if Cardinal fans thought this was to be the opening act in a rout of the great Philadelphia club, they were much mistaken. Grove would scatter eight hits over the next eight innings, mixed in with seven strikeouts, to keep the Cardinals off the scoreboard for the rest of the game. Pepper Martin had two of those eight hits, going three-for-four in the game and stealing a base, to set the tone for much of what would follow in the series.

Derringer retired the A's in order in the bottom of the second but got into trouble when he faced the bottom third of the Philadelphia lineup in the third inning. Jimmy Dykes led off with a single and moved to third on a line drive single to right by Dib Williams. Lefty Grove struck out, leaving the runners on first and third. Max Bishop then hit a ground ball that ended up being a fielder's choice when Dykes was tagged out at home plate. Mule Haas stepped into the batter's box with two outs and runners on first and second. Haas got into one and doubled, scoring Bishop to cut the Cardinal lead in half. Derringer then walked Mickey Cochrane to load the bases. A walk to Al Simmons forced in a run to tie the score and brought big Jimmie Fox to the plate with a chance to break things open. Foxx did not disappoint. A single to center brought Haas and Cochrane around to score, and the A's moved on top, 4–2. Bing Miller was the ninth Philadelphia batter in the inning. His ground out ended the A's rally, but not before giving Grove a lead he would not relinquish. Derringer gave up four more hits through the middle three innings but also fanned four A's batters in keeping Philadelphia from scoring again.

In the top of the seventh, Mickey Cochrane singled with one out. Al Simmons followed by crushing a Derringer pitch, driving it deep into the left field bleachers for a two-run homer that gave the A's a 6–2 lead. Syl Johnson came in to relieve Derringer in the eighth and did his job by holding the score where it was. Johnson retired all six batters he faced, giving his team a chance for a rally, but Grove made sure that didn't happen. Lefty got the Cardinals batters in order in the eighth before giving up a leadoff double to shortstop Charlie Gelbert in the ninth. Ray Blades came in to pinch-hit for Johnson, and Grove sat him down on strikes. Gus Mancuso was sent to the plate to bat for Andy High, and Grove got him to pop out on a foul ball to first baseman Jimmie Foxx. Wally Roettger then stepped into the batter's box as the last hope for the Cards. Roettger got hold of a Grove fastball and drove it deep to center field, but the ballpark held it and Haas made the catch to end the game. The A's had captured the 6–2 victory on the road, and so far, the series was going exactly as the experts had predicted it would.

One cause of concern for the Athletics was the physical condition of Grove. Lefty had developed a nasty blister on one of his throwing fingers that made it painful to throw his patented fastball efficiently. He mixed in a large number of curveballs and slower stuff, as he battled to keep the Cards hitters off-balance. His good control and the fact that he had issued no base on balls had kept him in the game. Following the decision, Grove was asked about his injured throwing hand. "Naw, the blister didn't hurt," he responded, "but them dinky hits they made got me mad. I started thinking that maybe my control was too good. You know I was putting them right over the plate. I started thinking, and you know what happens when a lefthander gets to thinking. Well, I began to chuck up slow ones and a little curve. Every time I tossed one the Cards got a hold of it. From now on, they won't see nuthin' but fastball pitching."[3] Lefty was not only a competitor, he was a warrior. He had been known to pitch before with blood oozing from blisters on his fingers without missing his spot in the rotation. His mental and physical toughness were not open to question, but he would need more than that to dominate a talented lineup of St. Louis hitters. He would need to be

EIGHT. *Facing the Cardinals Again*

in top form. The problem was he was battling a nagging injury that kept him from bringing the heat in his customary fashion, and he would need to depend more on his toughness than his talent in order to emerge triumphant over the Cards.

Game Two was played the following day, also at Sportsman's Park, in front of nearly 36,000 screaming St. Louis fans. George Earnshaw faced Bill Hallahan in what was one of the best pitching performances of the series. Hallahan pitched carefully to the Philadelphia lineup, allowing seven walks through nine innings of work. Mickey Cochrane and Jimmie Foxx were the recipients of four of the seven walks, as Hallahan determined not to let these two power hitters beat him with a long ball. He offset his high number of walks by giving up only three hits to the potent Philadelphia lineup and by striking out eight A's batters. Hallahan's performance held the A's scoreless through eight innings, and he snuffed out a potential rally in the ninth, when Philadelphia had two runners on with one out, by striking out the final two A's batters of the inning. The last strikeout did not end the inning, however. In one of the most bizarre plays to take place in World Series competition, Jimmy Moore struck out on a ball that hit the dirt before reaching the glove of Cardinals catcher Jimmie Wilson. Instead of throwing the ball to first to complete the strikeout, Wilson threw it to third baseman Jake Flowers. Flowers, thinking the game had ended, began to trot off the field with the ball in his grasp, obviously wanting a souvenir game ball to commemorate the win. Jimmy Moore was confused by the whole situation. The usually unflappable Connie Mack had come to the top of the dugout steps and was screaming at Moore to get to first. Moore didn't hear Mack, and finally realized what was going on when he saw third base coach Eddie Collins jumping up and down and waving his arms wildly. Moore got the message before Flowers, and he scampered to first base without a throw, loading the bases and forcing Hallahan to get a fourth out in the inning. Max Bishop followed with a chance to tie the game with a single. Hallahan got him to hit a weak foul pop out to first base to bring the fiasco to a close and end the potential Philadelphia rally.[4]

Earnshaw was up to the challenge. Scattering only six hits along with a single walk, he kept his team in the game by keeping the Cards off the scoreboard. The Cardinals broke on top with a run in the bottom of the second when Pepper Martin lined a one-out double to left field. Martin promptly stole third, and scored on a sacrifice fly to center off the bat of Jimmie Wilson. In the seventh, Martin led off the inning with a single, then swiped second to get in scoring position. He moved to third on a ground out by Wilson, and scored on a bunt by Charlie Gelbert. That was it for the scoring. The Cardinals had manufactured two runs playing small ball. Pepper Martin had not only scored both runs, he had made them possible with his larceny on the base paths, swiping his third base in the two games played. He was also five-for-seven at the plate thus far in the series, and had become an overnight sensation in St. Louis. The 2–0 decision evened the series, making it a best-of-five affair, as both teams took off two days for travel before resuming the contest in Philadelphia.

Burleigh Grimes, the thirty-seven-year-old spitball-throwing veteran, got the start against Lefty Grove in Game Three of the series, played at Shibe Park on October 5 in front of more than 32,000 Philadelphia fans. The spitball had been outlawed by the major leagues in 1920, but the ban had been grandfathered in, meaning that pitchers who had been throwing the pitch could continue to use it for the duration of their careers. Grimes, who debuted with the Pittsburgh Pirates in 1916, fell into this category and was still allowed to throw the wet one.[5]

The blister on Grove's throwing finger was still giving him trouble as he took the mound to face the Cardinals. Nevertheless, he used his curve and slow stuff to sit down St. Louis in order in the top of the first. Grimes responded by getting three straight in the A's half of the inning, and the game moved on to the second. After issuing a leadoff walk to Jim Bottomley, Lefty got Chick Hafey on a pop foul ball to Foxx. The red-hot Pepper Martin then came to the plate and promptly smacked a single to center, advancing Bottomley to third. Jimmie Wilson followed with a single to right, scoring Bottomley. Martin alertly moved to third, and came in to score on a sacrifice fly by Charlie Gelbert. The Cards put two more runs on the scoreboard in the top of the fourth when Martin followed Chick Hafey's leadoff single with a double that split the A's center and right fielders. Grove got the next two hitters out but surrendered a single to his mound opponent that drove in both base runners. The Cardinals had posted two runs in the second and fourth, and Pepper

EIGHT. Facing the Cardinals Again

Martin had been in the middle of both rallies. Grove was taken out of the game after eight innings, and Roy Mahaffey took the mound to begin the top of the ninth. Jake Flowers pinch-hit for starting third baseman Sparky Adams and led off the inning with a walk. He was erased on a bunt attempt by Wally Roettger that failed to advance him. Frankie Frisch grounded out to third, but Jim Bottomley picked up the base runner by belting a double to right-center that made the score 5–0.

In the meantime, Grimes was having it all his own way against the dreaded Philadelphia lineup. The A's were held hitless through seven innings, and didn't get to Grimes until Bing Miller roped a single to center in the eighth. In the bottom of the ninth, Mickey Cochrane coaxed a two-out walk from Grimes, one of four issued by the veteran that day. Al Simmons followed with an opposite-field homer to deep right field that finally got the A's on the board and made the score 5–2. Jimmie Foxx walked toward the plate, and the Philadelphia faithful held their breath, hoping this would be the beginning of another late-inning scoring binge like the one that had defeated the Cubs in the series two years ago. Foxx ended the suspense, though, by striking out to end the inning and give the Cardinals the 5–2 victory and a 2–1 lead in the series. Pepper Martin, who was rapidly becoming the biggest story in baseball, had once more plagued the A's by going two-for-four and scoring two runs in the game. On the plus side, it was the first game of the series in which he had not stolen a base.

In Game Four, played at Shibe Park on October 6, Connie Mack turned to George Earnshaw to stop the bleeding and get the team even in the series. Earnshaw had turned in an impressive performance in Game Two, allowing only six Cardinal hits, and Mack hoped he would have the same good stuff in this outing. The backup ace of the A's delivered more than was expected of him, as Earnshaw pitched one of his finest games of the year. Keeping the St. Louis batters constantly off stride, Earnshaw struck out eight while allowing only one free pass in nine innings of work. He restricted the Cards to only two hits, both of them to the irrepressible Pepper Martin, who went two-for-three in the game and stole another base. The A's got out to an early lead in the bottom of the first off St. Louis starter Syl Johnson, when Max Bishop led off with a single and was driven in two batters later when Al Simmons doubled. Johnson kept things close after that, keeping Philadelphia from scoring another run through five innings. Jimmie Foxx greeted Johnson with a two-out homer in the sixth, however. It was a crushing blow to left that didn't just score a run, it shattered the opposing pitcher's confidence. Bing Miller followed with a double, and Jimmy Dykes drove him in with a single to left. Dib Williams then singled to left, and Gabby Street had seen enough. Johnson was having too much trouble trying to get the third out of the inning, so Jim Lindsey was sent in to replace him, even though the next hitter in the lineup was George Earnshaw. Lindsey struck Earnshaw out to end the inning and the scoring for the day. Earnshaw made his three runs stand up in the 3–0 two-hit shutout that tied the series once more and made it a best-of-three championship.

Waite Hoyt got the start in the last game of the series to be played in Philadelphia on October 7. Bill Hallahan got the ball for the Cards, looking for another post-season win. In some ways, Hoyt was a natural choice for Mack to give the ball to for this big game. With ten World Series starts under his belt, the fourteen-year veteran had more post-season experience than any member of the Philadelphia staff.[6] The Cardinals struck early with a run in the top of the first. Sparky Adams led off with a single to left. Hoyt got George Watkins to fly out, then surrendered another single to Frankie Frisch, moving the lead runner to third. Pepper Martin's performance through four games had earned him a promotion, as Gabby Street elevated him to the cleanup position in the lineup. Martin strode to the plate and committed what was becoming an uncommon act for him—he made an out. He did drive the ball to deep left field, however, which allowed the runner on third to score. Even when the A's got him out, Martin found a way to torture them. And torture them he would on this day. Martin hit safely in his next three plate appearances of the game, crushed a two-run homer, and drove in four runs in a game he single-handedly took over. Hoyt did well over the first five innings, allowing only the single run in the first, but the A's were unable to get anything going in the form of run support. Hallahan retired the first twelve Philadelphia hitters in order until Al Simmons led off the fifth with a single. Jimmie Foxx then walked to give Philadelphia its first scoring threat of the game, but Hallahan got two foul pop-ups and a strikeout to stunt the A's rally before it really began.

EIGHT. Facing the Cardinals Again

Pepper Martin gave the Cardinals some breathing room with a two-run homer in the top of the sixth. Rube Walberg replaced Hoyt in the seventh, and Martin showed that he had no bias toward any particular Philadelphia pitcher by nailing him for a two-out single that drove in his fourth RBI of the game. Charlie Gelbert got a single in the top of the ninth to drive in Jim Bottomley with the only run of the game not attributed to Martin. The A's scored their only run of the game in the seventh, when Simmons and Foxx both singled, and Simmons came home on a ground ball force out by Bing Miller. Hallahan shut the door for the final three frames, shocking the A's and their faithful with the 5–1 loss that gave St. Louis a 3–2 lead in the series, with the final two games to be played back at Sportsman's Park. Though most baseball fans felt the A's could take two straight from any team in the game, and still predicted a third straight crown, St. Louis fans were now convinced that the postseries parties would be held in Missouri, not Pennsylvania.

After a day off for travel, the teams met on October 9 for the sixth game of the series. Philadelphia found itself in an unfamiliar position for the current team members. They were facing elimination. Connie Mack turned to Lefty Grove to keep the A's in the series and give them a chance to win it all in Game Seven. It would be a different Lefty Grove than the one who had lost Game Three in Philadelphia. The blister that had caused him so much trouble in his first two outings was healing nicely, and most of the pain that it had caused him in throwing his fastball was gone. An Associated Press sportswriter thought that he was "pitching at the very peak of his form for the first time in this intersectional warfare."[7] Having Lefty healthy again was indeed a boost for the A's, but the team was having other problems that made them look like the White Elephants John McGraw had tagged them to be so many years before. After scoring six runs in the series opener, the offense had gone on vacation, scoring a total of six more runs in the next four games. The team as a whole was batting .257 against St. Louis pitching, but that was skewed by Al Simmons' .350 average and the torrid .429 pace that Jimmie Foxx was setting. Mickey Cochrane was hitting a dismal .188. Mule Haas was batting only .167, and Max Bishop and Bing Miller were tied at .158. Jimmy Dykes was having a good series, batting .313, but the problem was that no one was getting on to set the table for Simmons, Foxx, or

Dykes. Many of the A's batters had come out of the gate slowly to start the season but had rebounded to record a .287 team batting average by the end of the year. It could only be hoped that their slow start in the series was also a passing phase that was about to come to an abrupt close.

Paul Derringer got the start for the Cardinals in Game Six, in a pitching rematch of the opener. Derringer pitched well, matching Lefty through four innings, with each pitcher allowing only a single hit. Things came unglued for the rookie in the top of the fifth, when Jimmie Foxx led off the inning and reached base on an error by the third baseman, Jake Flowers. Bing Miller then sacrificed Foxx to second before Jimmy Dykes walked. Dib Williams hit a single to right-center that brought Foxx around with the first run of the game. Derringer then struck out Grove for the second out of the inning, and with the light-hitting Max Bishop coming to the plate, it looked as if he would get off the hook with minimum damage. But Bishop walked to load the bases, then Mule Haas walked to force in a another run. Mickey Cochrane came to life, getting one of his few hits in the series, that drove in Williams. When Al Simmons took a base on balls to walk in another run, Derringer's day was done, and Syl Johnson came in to replace him. Johnson got Jimmie Foxx to pop out to the shortstop to end the inning. The A's had sent ten men to the plate, and had scored four runs, but they had done so with only two hits. An error and four walks had done the damage to the Cardinals, and all of the runs were unearned.

In the meantime, Grove was pitching a gem. He allowed only five Cardinal hits in a complete-game effort while striking out seven and walking only one. St. Louis got on the scoreboard in the bottom of the sixth when Jake Flowers hit a one-out double, advanced to third on a fly out by Roettger, and scored on a single by Frankie Frisch. The Cardinals only had one base runner the rest of the game, when Roettger struck out on a pitch in the dirt but reached base on an error by Cochrane. Grove was even able to shut down the A's biggest nemesis in the series, Pepper Martin, who went zero-for-three with a walk. Jim Lindsey came in to pitch for the Cardinals in the top of the seventh, and was greeted with another Philadelphia scoring barrage. Max Bishop led off the inning with a single to right, and was bunted to second by Mule

EIGHT. *Facing the Cardinals Again*

Haas. Mickey Cochrane flied out to left, and the team looked to Al Simmons for some two-out magic to bring another run home. Simmons delivered a single to center that scored Bishop, and Foxx followed with a single to left. Lindsey then hit Bing Miller with a pitch to load the bases. Jimmy Dykes worked Lindsey for a walk that brought Simmons home. When Dib Williams hit a fly ball to left fielder Chick Hafey, the inning should have been over, but Hafey misplayed the ball, allowing Williams to reach and Foxx and Miller to score. Lefty Grove was the ninth Philadelphia batter to come to the plate in the inning, and he grounded out to get Lindsey off the mound and into the dugout. The A's had scored four more runs on three hits. Hafey's error had accounted for two of the scores, both of which were unearned. The final score of 8–1 looked like the Philadelphia bats had finally awakened, but the reality was that only two of the runs were earned, and the A's could thank Cardinal errors for their large margin of victory.

The series came down to a winner-take-all game on October 10 at Sportsman's Park. Game Six had been watched by nearly 40,000 fans, as the Cardinal faithful hoped to see their team capture the title. Grove's performance served to dampen their enthusiasm, however, as only slightly more than half that number filed in to the stadium to see the deciding game. George Earnshaw got the nod from Connie Mack to start the all-important final contest. Earnshaw's two-hit shutout performance in Game Four probably factored heavily into the light turnout of St. Louis fans. Mack stated, "This is the first time I've even been in the seventh game of the World Series. But I think George will make everything right."[8] Burleigh Grimes would be his mound opponent on this day, as the spitball specialist sought to win his second victory of the series. Earnshaw pitched well, limiting the Cardinal hitters to four hits in seven innings of work. It appeared that the A's pitchers had finally figured out how to keep Pepper Martin from punishing them, as Earnshaw repeated Grove's feat of keeping the center field spark plug hitless in three official at-bats. Martin did reach base on one of the two walks issued by Earnshaw and promptly stole second on Cochrane to keep his name in contention as the best player in the series, but he neither scored nor drove in any runs. Ironically, he was still involved in the first run scored in the game by the Cardinals. Andy High led off the St. Louis half of the first with a single to left. George Watkins followed with another single in the same direction. Frankie Frisch laid down a sacrifice bunt that moved both runners ninety feet up the base paths, bringing Pepper Martin to the plate with a chance to do some early damage. Earnshaw issued a walk to Martin, but not before throwing a wild pitch that allowed High to trot home from third. Martin didn't stay on first base long. He swiped second, putting two runners in scoring position for the left fielder, Ernie Orsatti. When Orsatti struck out on a ball in the dirt, Cochrane completed the play by throwing to first. Watkins broke for the plate, and Jimmie Foxx's return throw to Cochrane sailed wildly, allowing the unearned run to score. By swiping second base, Martin had made it necessary for Cochrane to complete the strikeout of Orsatti by throwing to first, which had allowed Watkins to score. Even when they held Martin down, it seemed as if he still found a way to impact the game.

In the bottom of the third, the Cardinals got the other two hits that Earnshaw would allow in the game. High led off with a single, and Watkins followed with a two-run blast to deep right that gave the Cards a 4–0 lead. Earnshaw would exit the game after seven innings, as Rube Walberg came in to pitch the eighth to try to keep it close. Walberg gave up one hit, giving St. Louis a grand total of five for the day, and succeeded in keeping them from adding to their lead.

Earnshaw and Walberg had combined to pitch a fine game, but Grimes was outdueling them. The crafty veteran allowed only five hits and three walks through eight innings of work. Bishop, Haas, Cochrane, Foxx and Dykes had been held hitless, as Grimes put a choke hold on the Philadelphia offense. In the ninth inning, Al Simmons led off with a walk. Jimmie Foxx then fouled out to the catcher, and Bing Miller hit a grounder to the shortstop that forced Simmons at second. Grimes gave up a walk to Jimmy Dykes, and Dib Williams loaded the bases with a single to left. Connie Mack then sent Doc Cramer to the plate to bat for Walberg. Cramer came through with a single to center that scored Miller and Dykes, and the A's were back within striking distance. Max Bishop came to the plate batting about .150, but Gabby Street decided not to take any chances. It would be Bishop's fourth at-bat against Grimes, and the veteran pitcher was starting to tire, so Street brought in Bill Hallahan

EIGHT. *Facing the Cardinals Again*

to try to get the final out. Hallahan got Bishop to fly out to center to stun the Athletics and shock the baseball world.

Appropriately, it was Pepper Martin who caught the ball in center field to record the final out. It had been his series. Martin hit .500 in the seven games, collecting the most hits of any player on either team. He also had scored and driven in the most runs, and had swiped five bases. One sportswriter thought that Martin's play had been decisive in the series. He wrote that Martin "stole everything but the elephant's trunks and at the finish he had catcher Mickey Cochrane searching himself to find out if he still had his shoes."[9] Connie Mack's mighty Philadelphia squad had fallen to the Cardinals and would not win their record-setting third consecutive World Series. Little did any of them realize that the loss signaled not only the end of the series, but also the end of Philadelphia's dynasty in the major leagues. The A's would never return to the Fall Classic as long as they were in Philadelphia, and forty-one years later, when an Athletics team once again represented the American League in the World Series, they would hail from Oakland, California.

Lefty had done his part in the series, winning two of the three games he started, and ended the 1931 campaign with a combined regular and post-season record of 33–5. Though the campaign had not ended as expected for the team, Grove had experienced his finest year in the majors while putting together a season that would make him a legend in the game.

NINE
End of an Era

The 1931 season was the high-water mark for the Philadelphia Athletics, and the end of one of baseball's first dynasties. From 1929 through 1931, the A's compiled an envious record of 313–143, and scored a total of 2,710 runs while allowing 1,992 to their opponents. The better-known Yankees team of 1926–1928 had a record of 302–160, scored 2,716 runs, and gave up 1,997 runs. Both teams won three pennants and two World Series. Lefty Grove had the best three-year run of any player on either team. From 1929 through 1931, Lefty's record was 79–15, for a winning percentage of .840, the best run of the century, .067 better than the three-year run of the great Christy Mathewson, from 1908 through 1910.[1] The 1931 campaign proved to be the best season in Grove's illustrious career, as his thirty-one wins led all of baseball, as did his 2.06 ERA and 175 strikeouts. Lefty was recognized for his accomplishments by being voted American League Most Valuable Player by the Baseball Writers Association of America, the first time the award was presented by that body. In order to win the award, Grove had to beat out fellow nominees Al Simmons and Lou Gehrig. It is interesting to note that Grove's MVP award is the only one not on display at the Baseball Hall of Fame, in Cooperstown, New York. Lefty took his trophy home to Lonaconing, Maryland, where it was displayed for many years in the local high school trophy case. When officials from the Hall of Fame asked him to donate it to the museum's exhibition, Grove emphatically declined. It was his opinion that the people of Lonaconing deserved to see it whenever they desired, and he would not ship it off to New York. When Valley High School was torn down, the trophy, along with a collection of Grove memorabilia, needed a new home. In 2001, the collection found a permanent home in a small museum located within the

NINE. *End of an Era*

George's Creek Regional Library, on Main Street.[2] It is also interesting to note that the pitcher that stands atop Lefty's trophy is a right-handed player. The officials who commissioned the work had no idea at the time of its manufacture who would win the award and opted for a righthander. Ironically, possibly the greatest left-handed pitcher to ever play the game was honored with a trophy depicting a player throwing from the right side.

Following the conclusion of the season, several A's players were part of a traveling team of all-stars that went to Japan to play exhibition games against a Japanese all-star team. Lefty Grove, Al Simmons and Mickey Cochrane joined other notables like Lou Gehrig, Frankie Frisch, and Rabbit Maranville in playing a seventeen-game schedule against the Japanese team in multiple cities across the country. This was the first time that any all-star team from the major leagues had traveled together to play ball, and it was sponsored by the owner of a Tokyo newspaper to breed enthusiasm for the game in Japan. The U.S. team won all seventeen games handily, but it was the enthusiasm of the Japanese people and not the won-lost record that most impressed those involved. Baseball was rapidly becoming a favored pastime in Japan, and the tour of the American stars enflamed passion for the sport among the Japanese people, who treated Grove, Simmons, and their teammates like royalty. "Grovesan," as the Japanese called him, said it "was the time of our lives."[3] Lefty was even presented with an oversized glove by adoring Japanese fans as a symbol of their esteem. On the glove was painted the image of crossed American and Japanese flags.

Going into the 1932 season, Lefty Grove signed a new two-year contract for $50,000. That was big money for a team already paying hefty sums to the likes of Simmons, Foxx and Cochrane, especially since fan attendance and gate revenues had been declining significantly since the 1929 season. From a starting point of some 839,000 fans in 1929, the A's had slipped to 627,000 in 1931. Neither the Shibes nor Mack had personal wealth to cover monetary losses of the team. The A's needed to pay for themselves if the team was to survive in its current state, and the constant worry over declining revenues made that seem like wishful thinking. Mack had no way of knowing it when he signed Grove to the extension, but the team's finances were about to take a substantial downturn that would dictate the breakup of the once-proud squad, as attendance for the 1932 season plummeted to 405,000.

On the field, the A's did not show any lack of composure resulting from their loss in the series to St. Louis. The team was in contention for the pennant for most of the season, finishing second to the Yankees with a record of 94–60. New York had equaled Philadelphia's torrid pace of 107 victories from the previous year to run away with the pennant by the end of the season, however. The A's stars gave their fans plenty to root for, even though the team failed to reach post-season play. Lefty Grove had another fine campaign, going 25–10 with a 2.86 ERA. Al Simmons hit .322 and belted thirty-five home runs. Jimmie Foxx was the biggest star in Philadelphia in 1932, however, as he won the American League Triple Crown by batting .364, hitting 58 home runs, and driving in 169. Foxx's home run total was the most ever hit by a right-handed batter in a season, and only bad luck prevented his breaking Babe Ruth's single-season record. Two homers hit by Foxx were washed out in games called due to rain, and another five bounced off a fence that had been installed before the season at Sportsman's Park that had not been there in 1927 when Babe Ruth set the standard. Even so, Foxx's monster year earned him MVP honors for the American League, and he joined Grove as the second straight Athletic to receive the award. For the most part, the 1932 squad was composed of the same players that had made up the 1931 team. The poor fan turnout during the season meant all that was about to change.

Immediately following the 1932 season, Connie Mack made a move intended to bring some financial stability to the A's. Al Simmons, Mule Haas, and Jimmy Dykes were all sold to the Chicago White Sox for the sum of $100,000. With three of their top stars gone, and an aging Bing Miller seeing reduced playing time, the 1933 A's looked very different from the team that had given the Yankees fits for three straight years. The team slipped to 79–72 for the season, good for only a third-place finish in the league. One bright spot was Jimmie Foxx. "The Beast" had another monster season, winning the Triple Crown again with his .356 batting average, 48 home runs, and 163 RBIs. Foxx won his second consecutive MVP award, and the third in a row for the A's. Grove had another terrific season with a record of 24–8, though his ERA had

NINE. End of an Era

jumped to over 3.00 for the first time in six years. The 1933 campaign would be Grove's seventh straight 20-plus victory season, and it would also be the end of his streak. From 1927 through 1933, Grove had won 172 games while losing only 54. Grove was selected as one of the representatives of the American League in the first All-Star Game against the National League stars. Lefty pitched in the ninth inning, with the American League leading, 4–2. He faced only three batters, the last of whom was Tony Cuccinello. Grove served up three straight fastballs to Cuccinello to strike him out. Tony would state, "I've hit against Dazzy Vance and Van Mungo and I thought they were pretty swift, but I never saw anything like that Grove."[4] Philadelphia fans had been fortunate to be spectators to one of the greatest displays of pitching talent ever witnessed in the game, but that too was about to change. Fan attendance at Shibe Park in the 1933 season diminished to 297,000, forcing management to make even deeper cuts to its lineup to be able to keep the team solvent. On December 12, 1933, Mack sent Lefty Grove, Rube Walberg, and Max Bishop to the Boston Red Sox for two backup players and $125,000. He then sent Mickey Cochrane to the Detroit Tigers for second-line catcher Johnny Pasek and $100,000. Pasek was promptly bundled in a deal that sent George Earnshaw to the Chicago White Sox for catcher Charlie Berry and $20,000.[5] The mighty A's had been dismantled. Jimmie Foxx was the only remaining tie to the dynasty days of two short years ago.

The 1934 season reflected the exodus of star players from the A's team. Connie Mack's boys had their first losing season since 1924, posting a record of only 68–82, finishing in fifth place in the league. Jimmie Foxx was the only real star attraction still with the team, and though the absence of teammates like Simmons, Cochrane, Haas, Dykes, and Bishop meant that it was easier for opposing teams to pitch around him, Foxx still managed to put together a spectacular season. Hitting .334, he swatted 44 home runs and drove in 130 RBIs to make him one of the most-feared batters in the game. Attendance in 1934 improved slightly, to 305,000 fans. This increase was not because of the way the team was playing, but because the Blue Laws had been eased, and Sunday baseball was finally being allowed in Philadelphia.

Because of glaring holes at so many positions, Jimmie Foxx was pressed into service in several different roles during the 1935 campaign.

Foxx saw time at first and third, and did duty behind the plate catching, as he became the workhorse on a team in decline. Though the A's were still hitting at a respectable rate, gone were the days when Grove, Earnshaw and Walberg mowed down opposing hitters. The team ERA of 5.12 for the 1935 season was far too high for the Philadelphia batters to overcome. The team finished the year in last place, with a record of 58–91. It was the first of numerous years for the A's to be cellar-dwellers, and the Philadelphia fans seemed to know that the end had come. Gate attendance was a dismal 233,000. Jimmie Foxx was still a hot ticket, and he padded his reputation in 1935 by hitting .346 and leading the league with 36 home runs. Foxx's value prompted Connie Mack to part with the player he had once referred to a "the dandy of them all." In December of 1935 Foxx was sent to the Boston Red Sox, along with pitcher Johnny Marcum, for $150,000.[6] The last vestige of the once-proud A's was gone. With Grove, Walberg, and Bishop already on the Red Sox roster, Foxx's addition amounted to something of a reunion for the former Athletics players.

From 1936 through 1946, the Philadelphia Athletics finished in last place in the American League nine times and never finished higher than seventh. Twice during that stretch they lost an abysmal 105 games, and did not break a twelve-year losing streak until the 1947 season, when they finished in fifth place with a 78–76 record. In 1950, Connie Mack decided to retire as the team's manager after fifty years at the helm. The 88-year-old Mack compiled an enviable record during his time with the A's. Mack guided the team to five World Series championships through two different periods of dynasty. He set the major league record for managing 7,755 games, and also established the mark for both wins and losses as a manager with a record of 3,731–3,948. None of these standards have ever been seriously challenged.

The 1954 slate would be the last season for the Athletics in Philadelphia. Shibe Park was renamed Connie Mack Stadium to honor the retired 50-year manager of the team, but that was the only high point of the year. The team finished dead last in the league, with a record of 51–103, amid rumors that the franchise was about to be sold. The rumors proved to be true, as Arnold Johnson purchased the A's with the intention of moving the team to Kansas City, Missouri. Poor attendance over

NINE. End of an Era

the last couple decades motivated the American League owners to approve the move, and the Kansas City A's began play in the 1955 season.

The move to Kansas City did little to improve the team's performance on the field. More than 1.3 million fans came to see the Athletics during their first year in Kansas City, a franchise attendance record that was not broken by the team until 1982. But the team did little to repay its new fans for their passionate support. The A's lost 193 games in their first two seasons in Kansas City, significantly dampening the enthusiasm of the Missouri faithful. Attendance topped 1 million fans each of the first two years before experiencing a steady decline. Part of the reason for dismay among the Kansas City faithful stemmed from the fact that the A's had become a sort of minor league farm club for the New York Yankees. Numerous unfair trades were made in which talented young players, the likes of Clete Boyer, Hector Lopez, and Roger Maris, were sent to the Yankees in exchange for older players at the end of their careers, such as Billy Martin, Hank Bauer, and Don Larsen.[7] The fans quickly determined that team management was not trying to put a winning team on the field, and they showed their displeasure by not buying tickets to see the Athletics play. They weren't missing much. During their first five years in Kansas City, the Athletics finished in sixth place in the league in their inaugural campaign, followed by four years in last place or next to last. Their record over that span was an abysmal 313–456, and the closest they came to a successful season took place in 1958 when they finished 73–81.

In March of 1960, owner Arnold Johnson died from a cerebral hemorrhage. After the conclusion of the season, Charles O. Finley, who had earned a fortune in the insurance and real estate business, bought controlling interest in the team from the Johnson family, and the Athletics entered into a new era of their existence. The following year, Finley purchased complete interest in the club and became the sole owner. From the very start, Finley explored the possibilities of moving the team out of Kansas City, even though he publicly declared that the A's would remain a Missouri-based club. Behind the scenes, Finley privately sought moves to Texas and also tried to orchestrate a shift that would have moved the White Sox to Seattle, creating an opening in Chicago for his team. One positive feature of Finley's ownership was the fact that the A's were no longer a farm club for the Yankees. To demonstrate that fact, Finley purchased a bus, pointed it toward New York, and set it on fire. Young talent showing potential would be retained by the A's instead of being dealt to the Yankees, and over the next several years the team developed a stockpile of promising young players who would become stars in the game. By 1967, Finley had convinced the league to grant permission for him to move the team to the West Coast, and the Athletics would open the 1968 campaign as the Oakland A's. Kansas City A's fans would never get to see a winning team on the field, but the drafting and player development that had taken place in Missouri was soon to pay dividends in California.

The 1968 team featured a number of youngsters that were soon to become stars of the game, including starting position players Reggie Jackson, Rick Monday, Joe Rudi, Bert Campaneris, Sal Bando, and Dave Duncan. The starting rotation was anchored by twenty-two-year-old Jim "Catfish" Hunter and twenty-three-year-old John "Blue Moon" Odom. An interesting tie to the team's former days of dynasty was Lew Krausse Jr., whose father pitched for the 1931 squad and witnessed the end of the A's dominance in the league. Lew Krausse Jr. pitched in thirty-six games for the A's in 1968 in a season that would see the team position itself for another run at greatness. A newcomer in 1968 who would appear in only one game was Roland "Rollie" Fingers, another bright star of the future. But the immediate star of the team was Hunter, who pitched a perfect game on May 8, the first perfect outing to be notched in the American League since 1922, when Charlie Robertson achieved the feat.[8] The A's were competitive for the first time in more than a generation, and finished the season with a record of 82–80.

The 1969 A's added catcher Gene Tenace to their lineup, as well as veteran outfielder Felipe Alou, and improved on their previous season record by finishing second in the American League West with an 88–74 mark. The 1970 squad finished the season with an almost identical record of 89–73, and was once again second in the American League West. The A's seemed poised to make another run at greatness, and needed only one or two more players to become real pennant contenders. Little did anyone realize in 1970 that the missing piece was already with the team.

NINE. End of an Era

A twenty-year-old rookie by the name of Vida Blue had made his debut that season. Blue pitched in only six games that year, but he went 2–0 with a 2.09 ERA that gave great promise of things to come. The A's were about to make another run at dynasty, and they would do it once more with an outstanding rotation of pitching talent.

In 1971, the A's won the American League West with a record of 101–60, and earned the right to play in the postseason for the first time in forty years. As in the old days, they did it with superior pitching and clutch hitting. Vida Blue was a sensation, with a record of 24–8, a minuscule ERA of 1.82, and 301 strikeouts. His spectacular season earned him both the Cy Young award and the American League Most Valuable Player award. Catfish Hunter kicked in twenty-one wins of his own, with a 2.96 ERA. Reggie Jackson, Sal Bando and Rick Monday harkened back to the glory days of Simmons, Foxx and Cochrane by belting 74 home runs, and the team as a whole accounted for 160 round-trippers. Though the team was swept by the Baltimore Orioles in the American League Championship Series, baseball experts around the country knew the A's were a team whose time had come.

The next A's dynasty would be initiated with the 1972 season. The team took a step back from 1971, finishing with a record of 93–62, which was still good enough to win the American League West. Vida Blue took a huge step backward, finishing the year with a disappointing 6–10 record despite a superior 2.80 ERA. Catfish Hunter had his second straight season with more than twenty wins, posting a 21–7 record with an ERA of 2.04. Blue Moon Odom went 15–6, while newly acquired Ken Holtzman had a record of 19–11 with a 2.51 ERA. The team would go on to win the pennant in a five-game series with the Detroit Tigers, earning the right to play the Cincinnati Reds in the World Series. The Reds were favored in the series, but the A's prevailed in a hard-fought classic that went the full seven games. For the sixth time in franchise history, the Athletics stood atop the baseball world, and they were just beginning.

The team defended its title in 1973 by winning the American League West for the third straight year with a record of 94–68. Pitching once more led the way, as Vida Blue, Catfish Hunter, and Ken Holtzman all recorded twenty or more wins, reminiscent of the Grove, Earnshaw, and Walberg rotation of 1931. Reggie Jackson swatted thirty-two home runs, closely followed by Sal Bando's twenty-nine and Gene Tenace's twenty-four. The A's topped the Baltimore Orioles in a five-game American League Championship Series to earn the right to play the New York Mets in the World Series. As with the previous year, the series went the full seven games, and the A's had to come from behind to win the final two contests to repeat as world champions. Reggie Jackson came through with big run-producing clutch hits in each of the final two games, and was well on his way to establishing himself as "Mr. October."

The 1974 season placed the latest version of the Athletics in the same position their predecessors found themselves in some forty-three years earlier. The gutty A's were favored to repeat as American League West champions and put themselves in a position to accomplish what the 1931 team could not by winning a third consecutive title. Once again, pitching led the way, as Catfish Hunter had the best season of his career, leading the league with twenty-five wins and an ERA of 2.49. Hunter won the Cy Young award for that year, and led the team into the playoffs in much the same manner that Lefty Grove had in 1931. For the third time in four years, the A's met the Baltimore Orioles in the American League Championship Series. The Orioles surprised the baseball world in game one by hitting Hunter hard to take the game, 6–3. But the A's bounced back to win the next three games, earning their third straight pennant and the chance to play the Los Angeles Dodgers in the Fall Classic. Pitching prevailed, as Catfish Hunter, Ken Holtzman, Blue Moon Odom, and Rollie Fingers combined to hold the Dodgers to ten runs in five games, limiting the Los Angeles club to two scores in each of the contests. The A's scored only sixteen runs in the series, but that was good enough to win the championship. It was a return to dynasty for the Athletics, as they sat atop the baseball world once more as the undisputed best in the game. The 1974 squad achieved what the 1931 team had not. The 1931 team could have been the first club in baseball history to win three consecutive championships. By the time the 1974 A's accomplished the feat, the New York Yankees had already done it. Nevertheless, the A's became only the second team to three-peat as World Series champs, earning their rightful place as one of the best franchises in the game. The A's would go on to appear in three consecutive World Series from 1988–1990, but they would only capture the title in 1989. The team's

NINE. *End of an Era*

nine World Series championships rank third all-time, behind the twenty-seven held by the Yankees and the eleven won by the St. Louis Cardinals. The winning tradition established by Connie Mack and stars like Pennock, Bender, Simmons, Foxx and Grove is proudly evident in the A's teams of this generation. Baseball has a way of doing that. Past and present are always combined in our national pastime, as the stars of the present compete against the ghosts of the past, as well as against their peers. It is part of the rich history that serves to make baseball the grand game it is, and America's pastime.

Epilogue

The 1931 Philadelphia Athletics were one of the best teams to ever grace a baseball diamond. The members of that team forged a dynasty as enviable as any in professional sports, and in the process, earned a legendary status in the game. From 1929–1931, the Athletics had a combined record of 313-143. They scored 2,710 runs, while allowing 1,992 to the competition. The 1926–1928 New York Yankees, by comparison, had a record of 302-160, scored 2,716 runs and gave up 1,997.[1] That amounts to a one-run difference between the two teams, as both captured three pennants and won two World Series crowns. Connie Mack's boys forged one of the greatest runs at dynasty in the history of baseball, and in doing so, cemented their place as some of the best players in the history of the game. No one can tell what might have happened if not for the economic difficulties of the time, which forced the disbandment of this powerful squad at the peak of its baseball prowess. Had the Great Depression not intervened to put an end to their dominance, the Philadelphia Athletics, already the class of the major leagues, might have gone on to add to their legend and supplant the New York Yankees as the greatest franchise of all-time. To be sure, this is only speculation, but the career achievements of players like Grove, Cochrane, Simmons, and Foxx after leaving Philadelphia would seem to state that had that team been allowed to carry forward, it would have remained one of the most fearsome lineups in either league. But baseball is both a business and a game, and in the case of the Philadelphia Athletics, lack of money and waning attendance caused the business portion of the equation to take precedence over the game, as the once-proud A's were dismantled, their greatest stars sent to steal the limelight in other cities.

Connie Mack continued to be the face of the franchise until 1954, when the club was sold and moved to Kansas City. He holds the record for managerial service with fifty years at the helm of the A's. He was the first manager to win three World Series titles, and is the only skipper to win consecutive crowns on separate occasions (1910–11, 1929–30). His five World Series titles rank first among managers, and his nine American League pennants place him second all-time. The venerable old Mack was a baseball wizard who recognized raw talent and knew how to get the most out of it. Never one to over-manage a game, Mack put his pieces in place and allowed his players to play the game. His steady guidance served to give direction to both his team as a whole and to his individual players and earned him the respect and admiration of baseball fans everywhere. He was both anchor and inspiration for his players, knew how to keep them grounded and how to get the most out of them. Even the irascible Lefty Grove looked upon him as a sort of father figure. For his part, Mack viewed Lefty as one would an erring child in need of direction. "I took more from Grove than I would from any other man living," Mack once stated near the end of Lefty's career. "He said things and did things. But he's changed. I've seen it come, year by year. He's got to be a great fellow."[2] Mack used his calm demeanor to guide the careers of numerous players whose footsteps were placed on the path to stardom through his insight and wisdom. Pennock, Bender, Collins, Simmons, Cochrane, Foxx, and Grove are but a sampling of the young men whose lives he touched on the baseball diamond and beyond. He would be elected to the Baseball Hall of Fame in 1937, thirteen years before giving up the helm of his beloved athletics. In the years that followed, his plaque at Cooperstown would be surrounded by many familiar faces he had both managed and competed against. Connie Mack died on February 8, 1956, at the age of ninety-three. He is buried in the Holy Sepulchre Cemetery in Cheltenham, Pennsylvania.

Al Simmons played twelve of his twenty major league seasons with the A's. In 1933, when Connie Mack sent him off to the Chicago White Sox, his career batting average was a lofty .356, he had swatted 209 home runs, and had driven in 1,179. After three years with the White Sox, Simmons would play for the Tigers, Senators, Braves, Reds and Red Sox before his illustrious career ended. In 1944, he found himself right back where he started, playing for Mack and the A's. At the age of forty-two,

Epilogue

his signing was more out of respect for his past achievements than for his ability to help the club. It also allowed one of the greatest A's of all-time to retire as a member of the Philadelphia team where he had gained his greatest fame. Simmons appeared in only four games that season, and came to the plate but six times. He managed to rap out three hits in those at-bats, however, retiring with an average of .500 for the year. After his playing days concluded, Simmons served as a coach for Connie Mack from 1945–49, before becoming a coach for the Indians in 1950. Al Simmons was elected to the Baseball Hall of Fame in 1953 in what was amazingly his seventh year of eligibility. He died on May 26, 1956, at his home in Milwaukee, Wisconsin, from a heart attack. Simmons was buried in the St. Adalbert's Cemetery in Milwaukee.

Mickey Cochrane played nine years for the Athletics before being sent to the Detroit Tigers to become their player-manager for the 1934 season. He would hit .320 that year, win the American League MVP award, and lead the Tigers into post-season play to face the St. Louis Cardinals. The Tigers would lose the series in seven games but would return the following year behind their on-field captain to face the Chicago Cubs. Cochrane would win his third World Series ring, as the Tigers defeated the Cubs in six games. Cochrane would continue to provide thrills for the Chicago fans until 1937. On May 25 of that year, Cochrane's baseball career came to a sudden end. Bump Hadley threw a pitch high and tight that struck Cochrane in the head, hospitalizing him for seven days and nearly taking his life. Doctors warned Cochrane against playing baseball again, so he confined his activities to managing the team. The inability to play caused his fiery nature to become subdued, however, and Mickey didn't take to just managing. He was replaced in the middle of the 1938 season and retired from the game. His lifetime batting average of .320, his two MVP awards, and his reputation as being one of the finest defensive catchers to ever play the game made Cochrane a sure bet to be elected to the Baseball Hall of Fame, and he received that honor in 1947, in the fifth year of his eligibility. Despite his head injury, Cochrane served in the U.S. Navy during World War II. Cochrane's old teammate, George Earnshaw, also entered the navy during the war, rising to the rank of Commander. After the war, Mickey went into the automobile business, running a car lot till the mid–1950s.

Epilogue

He died of lymphatic cancer in Lake Forest, Illinois, on June 28, 1962. According to his wishes, he was cremated, and had his ashes scattered over Lake Michigan.

Jimmie Foxx played the first eleven years of his twenty-year career with Philadelphia. In 1936, he became the last of the core group of players who had propelled the A's to dynasty to depart from the team, when he was sent to play for rival Boston. In his seven years with the Red Sox, Foxx would belt 222 home runs, and would win his third American League MVP award. Foxx would end his playing days with a whopping total of 534 home runs and a .325 batting average. At the time of his retirement, Foxx's home run total was second only to Babe Ruth, and his record of twelve consecutive seasons with thirty or more home runs stood until 2004, when it was broken by Barry Bonds. He worked as a minor league manager and coach for several years, including a stint as the manager of the Fort Wayne Daisies of the All-American Girls Professional Baseball League. In 1958, he retired from baseball, settling in Lakewood, Ohio. Bad investments caused him to be broke at the time of his retirement, and he was forced to take a job with the Lakewood Recreational Department. Foxx was inducted into the Baseball Hall of Fame in 1951, in his first year of eligibility. He died on July 21, 1967, in Miami, Florida, as a result of choking on a piece of food. Foxx was buried at the Flagler Memorial Park in Miami.

An argument could be made that Lefty Grove served as the catalyst that propelled an already-talented team to becoming a dynasty of champions. The first nine of his seventeen years on the mound were in Philadelphia. Over that time, he compiled a record of 195–79, with an ERA of 2.88 and 1,523 strikeouts. He led the league in wins four times, in strikeouts seven years in a row, and held the league's lowest ERA for a record nine years. From 1929–1931, when the A's climbed to the top of the baseball world, Grove posted an astounding record of 79–15, on his way to becoming the most dominant pitcher in the game. Grove was sold to the Red Sox for the 1934 campaign. He finished a disappointing 8–8 that year but rebounded in 1935 to post a 20–12 record with an impressive 2.70 ERA. During his eight years in Boston, Lefty was forced to rely more and more on his curveball, as his fastball began to lose much of its stuff. The 1941 season would prove to be his final campaign,

Epilogue

as Grove went 7–7, with a 4.37 ERA, and his twenty-one appearances were the fewest of his major league career. Red Sox owner Tom Yawkey felt that Grove still had a few good seasons left in his arm, but Lefty felt otherwise. His .500 record and high ERA had convinced him that the time had come to hang up his spikes and retire. Besides, his last victory of the 1941 campaign had lifted him to 300 career wins, placing him in select company in baseball history. Grove traveled to South Carolina in December of 1941 to go duck hunting with Yawkey on his plantation. The date was December 7, and as Yawkey remembered it, Lefty announced his decision to retire at approximately 11:00 a.m. By the time the pair returned to the hunting lodge, the news of the star lefthander's retirement paled beside the early reports of the Japanese sneak attack on Pearl Harbor that were just coming in. Grove returned to his home in Lonaconing, where he privately showed his personal feelings about the sinister act. Several years before, Lefty had been part of a team of major league all-stars that had toured Japan and played numerous exhibition games. Lefty was adored by the Japanese fans, who presented him with an oversized glove bearing crossed American and Japanese flags. Grove took a knife and scratched off the Japanese flag in a moment of anger. He could still be destructive when his dander was up. At forty-two years of age, he was too old for the service, but his son, Robert G. Grove, served as a radio operator in a tank destroyer unit, seeing combat in the European Theater of Operations.[3]

Upon retiring, Lefty returned to his beloved hometown of Lonaconing. In reality, he had never left. He would be spending his summers there now, as well as his winters. Grove spent more time at Lefty's Place, a combination pool hall, bowling alley and snack shop he had opened in 1929 as a place for locals to gather and socialize. Grove was found there often when he was not hunting, fishing, or working in his garden. Lefty's Place also served as a sort of baseball shrine in Lonaconing. Autographed pictures of greats like Babe Ruth, Lou Gehrig and Connie Mack adorned the walls, and Lefty kept almost 250 game balls from his playing days there. In a bat rack in his store room, there were autographed bats from most of the Hall of Fame players from the era. While Lefty loved to talk about baseball, he did not seem to regret his decision to retire from the game. One reason was his absolute disdain for large cities and

Epilogue

their hustle and bustle. He was much more at home in Lonaconing, where he was "Bob" to most of his friends and neighbors, not "Lefty." Always competitive, he would watch as a patron shot a good game of pool or rolled up a high score at bowling. Richard Grandstaff remembers that he often rewarded a good game or shot with an approving tweek on the neck or cheek of the patron.

While most residents of Lonaconing felt that he mellowed with age, Lefty never lost his fiery, competitive spirit. David Solosko, a resident of my hometown in Salisbury, Pennsylvania, and a left-handed pitcher on the local team, was taken by his mother, Evelyn, to meet Grove when David was a teenager intent upon becoming a major league ball player. Grove signed a baseball for David that is still one of his most-prized possessions, and talked to the lad a little about the game. Solosko freely admits that he was too much in awe of his boyhood hero to remember much of what Lefty said, but one thing stuck with him. Lefty eyed the teenager up and down before gruffly stating that he would never become a major league ball player. "You're too short and scrawny!" Grove stated, as he quashed David's boyhood dreams.[4] Solosko would go on to become a doctor, and just like the Moonlight Graham character in the movie *Field of Dreams*, would serve humanity through a lifetime spent in the field of medicine. But just like Moonlight Graham, Solosko would never forget his love of the game of baseball. The treasured keepsake of Lefty Grove's signed baseball was always kept in his desk at the numerous offices he used throughout his career.

Though Lefty claimed that he did not miss playing, he never strayed far from the game he loved. Whether it be supporting local youth baseball teams, listening to major league games on the radio, or attending old-timers events, Grove kept in close touch with the passion that had been a driving force in his life since his youth. In 1947, he was elected to the Baseball Hall of Fame on the third ballot, which was the beginning of frequent visits to Cooperstown to rub elbows and trade stories with other greats of the game. Ken Smith, director of the Baseball Hall of Fame, said that "Lefty was always faithful in his attendance at the Hall of Fame Day," an event held each summer as a time for the baseball greats to get together. "He showed up every year and was great company."[5] In 1969, he was named the best living left-handed pitcher in baseball (Bob Feller was named the best righthander), and Lefty made a trip to Washington, DC to be honored by President Richard Nixon.[6]

Lefty's life in Lonaconing was much the same as any other resident despite his celebrity status. In the late 1950s he was elected to the Lonaconing Town Council, and he also served for a time as the local chief of police. He also suffered from some of the same mistakes and misfortunes that plague everyone. In the early 1950s, Lefty and Ethel divorced due to his involvement with another woman. Though they continued to make trips together to a cabin Lefty owned for outings with their granddaughter, Lynn, the couple never reconciled. Lefty moved into a room next to the Republican Club, close to Lefty's Place. His granddaughter said, "The divorce was his one main regret. He never stopped loving her, and when she died, it nearly killed him." Ethel would die of coronary thrombosis in 1960, and Lefty visited her many times in the hospital before her passing.[7] Lefty was also suffering financial problems at this time. He played baseball at a time when the league offered no pension programs, his investments had not panned out as expected, and much of what he did have was lost in his divorce with Ethel. In 1961, these financial considerations caused him to move to Norwalk, Ohio, to live with his son, Bobby, and his wife, Jean. When Bobby and Jean separated in the mid–1960s, Grove continued to live with his daughter-in-law, who considered him family and called him "Dad." His world was devastated in 1972 when Bobby died at a young age from the same disease that had killed his mother. Lefty continued to live with Jean, and could usually be found in a rocking chair with two radios and a television keeping track of three different baseball games during the season. On May 22, 1975, he had gone downstairs to watch television in his rocking chair. There was no response when the housekeeper announced that dinner was ready, so she went to investigate. She found him dead from a heart attack, sitting peacefully with his hands on the chair and an extinguished cigar in his lap.[8]

Grove's body was taken back to Lonaconing, where funeral rites were held at the local Presbyterian church. The Reverend F. Blaine Rinker of the Midland Methodist Church performed the ceremony, as he had for Lefty's son a couple years earlier. Ken Smith, the director of the Baseball Hall of Fame, was in attendance, along with a couple hun-

Epilogue

dred other mourners who came to pay their respects. Among the floral tributes were those from Bowie Kuhn, the commissioner of Major League Baseball, Lee MacPhail, the president of the American League, and baseball great Ted Williams, who played with Lefty in his final year in the bigs. Lefty was laid to rest in Frostburg Memorial Park in Frostburg, Maryland, beside Ethel. A somewhat plain tombstone merely lists the family name of "Grove" across the top. Beneath that, Ethel's name in carved on the left. On the right, there is no mention of Lefty or to baseball. It simply says "Father- Robert M." Grove would leave the world in the same manner he had entered it, as a simple, common resident of Lonaconing.

With his passing, baseball lost one of the greatest pitchers ever to play the game. Indeed, there are many who feel that Lefty Grove was the greatest of them all. To be sure, Lefty felt that he deserved to be in that conversation. Once when he was in his seventies, he was known to have made the remark that he could still strike out a major league player. When reminded of his advanced age, Lefty retorted that age didn't matter. "They know my reputation." Know it they did. For a couple generations of baseball fans, Lefty Grove was considered to be simply the best in the game.

Appendix 1: Athletics 1931 Team and Individual Statistics

The pennant-winning 1931 Philadelphia Athletics were a fearsome offensive club that could score runs in bunches, and had the potential to knock the ball out of the park on any pitch. Hitters like Mickey Cochrane, Al Simmons, and Jimmie Foxx were the terror of opposing pitchers and the stuff of baseball legends. Even so, it was their pitching that made the A's champions and carried the team to its third consecutive American League title.

The Athletics' team batting average in 1931 was .287, good for third place in the league, behind New York and Cleveland. Their 858 runs scored was also a third-place finish behind the same two teams, with the Yankees putting up a first-place total of 1,067, for a 1.3 runs-per-game average better than the A's. While their 118 home runs earned them a second-place finish in the standings, it was only about three-quarters of the 155 slugged by the Yankees. Their 1,544 hits ranked fourth in the league, but they were next-to-last when it came to at-bats. In fact, the only thing the A's hitters paced the circuit during the 1931 season was getting hit by pitches. In that dubious category they led the league with 35 batters getting plunked. Bing Miller led the club, being hit ten times, while Jimmy Dykes reached base by taking one for the team six times.

Individual stats for the year saw Al Simmons lead the league with a batting average of .390 while swatting 22 home runs. He led the team in hits with 200, and his 128 RBIs and 13 triples were also team highs.

Appendix 1

Mickey Cochrane belted a lofty .349 for the season, adding 17 home runs and 31 doubles to the pot. Jimmie Foxx rebounded strongly from a poor start of the season to finish with a batting average of .291. He led the team with 30 home runs, and his 120 RBIs were second only to Simmons. Nearly 50 percent of his hits that season went for extra bases, as Foxx put on a display of power that would come to define his career. Mule Haas finished the campaign with a healthy .323 batting average and 82 runs scored. Max Bishop did his part in setting the table for the big bats in the middle of the order by hitting .294 and having an on-base average of .426, second-best on the team. A superior discipline at the plate led to 120 walks, by far the most on the team. His ability to reach safely paid dividends, as he led the club with 115 runs scored for the season. Bing Miller was a solid contributor with a .281 batting average and an ability to put the ball in play. His 16 strikeouts for the season were the lowest by far on the team, and represented a ratio of one strikeout in more than thirty-three at-bats. Jimmy Dykes hit a respectable .273, and while he did not have a lot of over-the-fence power, his 28 doubles helped to drive in 46 runs. Dib Williams was the lightest hitter of the starters, batting just .269 for the campaign, but like Miller he was a contact hitter that usually put the ball in play. Other notable contributors to the offensive lineup were Eric McNair, whose .271 batting average was good enough to have made him a starter on most other teams. Doc Cramer hit .260 during his stints in the outfield spelling the starters, while Joe Boley managed only .228 in relief of Dib Williams at short and in pinch-hitting roles. Overall, it was an impressive record for the American League champions, and the statistics were such that any team would wish to copy them at the beginning of a season. But the offensive power of the Athletics was not strong enough to propel the team to its third straight pennant. Instead, the strength was the dominant performance turned in by the team's pitching staff.

Philadelphia pitchers combined to lead the American League in wins (107), ERA (3.47), complete games (97), and shutouts (12), while allowing the fewest hits (1,342), runs (626), and earned runs (526). The team ranked third in strikeouts with 574 and gave up the second-fewest walks with 457. Their only weak category was in the 73 home runs allowed, which placed them fourth in the league, but fastball power pitchers tend to give up their share of long balls. Forty-two of the round-trippers were hit off Grove, Walberg and Earnshaw.

The A's staff was led by the Triple Crown performance of their ace, Lefty Grove. The big southpaw led the majors in wins with 31 and topped the bigs with his 2.06 ERA and winning percentage of .886. Lefty's 175 strikeouts were best in the American League, while his 62 walks were lowest among the big three starters on the staff and amounted to a free pass every 4⅔ innings. Surely, Grove was the catalyst for the Athletics' 1931 season, and it could be argued that without him the team would have had a mediocre year and finished well back in the pack. A workhorse as a starter and reliever, Grove logged twenty-seven complete games during the season, more than most modern-day pitchers accumulate in a career. George Earnshaw turned in a superior year with 21 wins and a .750 winning percentage. His 3.67 ERA was respectable and well below the league average. Earnshaw's 152 strikeouts made him one of the league leaders, while his 75 walks served as a testament to his control and his twenty-three complete games proved his endurance. Rube Walberg completed the trio of twenty-plus game winners from Philadelphia, kicking in 20 wins over the course of the campaign. His 3.74 ERA was respectable, as were his 106 strikeouts, but big Rube got into trouble at times with the free passes. Walberg led the team with 109 walks, and his 121 earned runs were also tops on the team, as opposed to the 66 Lefty allowed during his outings. But Walberg ate up innings. His 291 innings pitched led the team, representing three more than Grove and ten more than Earnshaw.

Other notable contributors were Eddie Rommel, whose 2.97 ERA was second best on the staff but would only earn him a 7–5 record for the year. Roy Mahaffey and Waite Hoyt provided the team with a much-needed boost in the second half of the season after both Earnshaw and Walberg dropped off the torrid pace with which they had begun the campaign. Mahaffey finished with a 15–4 record and an enviable .789 winning percentage, even though his ERA was 4.21. Hoyt went 10–5 for the A's after being acquired from Detroit, and while his 4.22 ERA was not up to the standard that had made him an ace of the Yankees teams of the 1920s, he won some big games for Philadelphia that helped them keep rolling during the summer of 1931. Hank McDonald started ten

Appendix 1

games for the A's that season and posted a respectable ERA of 3.71, but his 2–4 record made him one of only three pitchers on the roster with a losing mark. Four other pitchers saw service during the year: Jim Peterson, Bill Shores, Lew Krausse, and Sol Carter. They threw for a combined total of 42⅓ innings and went 1–4 for the season.

As good as the Philadelphia hitters were, the Athletics' pitchers were better, and with one of the finest pitching staffs ever assembled, it was the work off the mound that gave the team its third straight American League title and a chance to become the first team in baseball history to win three consecutive World Series crowns. In an era of the game best known for its offensive players like Babe Ruth, Lou Gehrig, Ty Cobb, Rogers Hornsby, Mel Ott, and Frankie Frisch, the big three of the Athletics' pitching staff emerged as a dominant force. Babe Ruth and Lefty Grove were not particularly friendly toward one another as a result of numerous face-to-face meetings on the field and the competitive spirit both men had. All the same, Lefty acknowledged the greatness of the man, and grudgingly paid tribute to all the hitters of his era in 1961 when he was evaluating the current crop of players. "They still hustle," Grove said, "but I don't see any Ty Cobbs or Tris Speakers or Babe Ruths. Ty Cobb could beat a club all by himself if you got him mad." Ruth once quipped about George Earnshaw, "I used to send a taxicab to the Almanac Hotel the day he was gonna pitch. I didn't want him to get lost on the way to the stadium," referring to the fact that he enjoyed hitting against Earnshaw. The fact is, Ruth had his greatest success against Philadelphia when he faced Rube Walberg. Ruth took Walberg deep for seventeen home runs over the course of his career, the most he hit off any pitcher who faced him.[1]

Appendix 2: Hall of Fame Players from the Golden Era (1925–1941)

National League: 42

Pete Alexander (pitcher) 1911–1930
Dave Bancroft (shortstop) 1915–1930
Jim Bottomley (first baseman) 1922–1937
Max Carey (outfielder) 1910–1929
Kiki Cuyler (outfielder) 1921–1938
Dizzy Dean (pitcher) 1930, 1932–1941, 1947
Frankie Frisch (second baseman) 1919–1937
Burleigh Grimes (pitcher) 1916–1934
Chick Hafey (outfielder) 1924–1935, 1937
Jesse Haines (pitcher) 1918, 1920–1937
Gabby Hartnett (catcher) 1922–1941
Billy Herman (second baseman) 1931–1943, 1946–1947
Rogers Hornsby (second baseman) 1915–1937
Carl Hubbell (pitcher) 1928–1943
Travis Jackson (shortstop) 1922–1936
George Kelley (first baseman) 1915–1917, 1919–1930, 1932
Chuck Klein (outfielder) 1928–1944
Fred Lindstrom (third baseman) 1924–1936
Ernie Lombardi (catcher) 1931–1947
Rabbit Maranville (shortstop) 1912–1933, 1935
Rube Marquard (pitcher) 1908–1925
John McGraw (manager) 1899, 1901–1932
Bill McKechnie (manager) 1915, 1922–1926, 1928–1946
Joe Medwick (outfielder) 1932–1948
Johnny Mize (first baseman) 1936–1942, 1946–1953

Appendix 2

Stan Musial (outfielder) 1941–1944, 1946–1963
Mel Ott (outfielder) 1926–1947
Pee Wee Reese (shortstop) 1940–1942, 1946–1958
Eppa Rixey (pitcher) 1912–1917, 1919–1933
Wilbert Robinson (manager) 1902, 1914–1931
Eddie Roush (outfielder) 1913–1929, 1931
Enos Slaughter (outfielder) 1938–1942, 1946–1959
Billy Southworth (manager) 1929, 1940–1951
Casey Stengel (manager) 1934–1936, 1938–1943, 1949–1960, 1962–1965
Bill Terry (first baseman) 1923–1936
Pie Traynor (third baseman) 1920–1935, 1937
Dazzy Vance (pitcher) 1915, 1918, 1922–1935
Lloyd Waner (outfielder) 1927–1942, 1944–1945
Paul Waner (outfielder) 1926–1945
Zack Wheat (outfielder) 1909–1927
Hack Wilson (outfielder) 1923–1934
Ross Youngs (outfielder) 1917–1926

American League: 47

Luke Appling (shortstop) 1930–1943, 1945–1950
Earl Averill (outfielder) 1929–1941
Chief Bender (pitcher) 1903–1917, 1925
Lou Boudreau (shortstop) 1938–1952
Ty Cobb (outfielder) 1905–1928
Mickey Cochrane (catcher) 1925–1937
Eddie Collins (second baseman) 1906–1930
Earle Combs (outfielder) 1924–1935
Stan Coveleski (pitcher) 1912, 1916–1928
Joe Cronin (shortstop) 1926–1945
Bill Dickey (catcher) 1928–1943, 1946
Joe DiMaggio (outfielder) 1936–1942, 1946–1951
Bobby Doerr (second baseman) 1937–1944, 1946–1951
Red Faber (pitcher) 1914–1933
Bob Feller (pitcher) 1936–1941, 1945–1956
Rick Ferrell (catcher) 1929–1945, 1947
Jimmie Foxx (first baseman) 1925–1942, 1944–1945
Lou Gehrig (first baseman) 1923–1939
Charlie Gehringer (second baseman) 1924–1942
Lefty Gomez (pitcher) 1930–1943
Joe Gordon (second baseman) 1938–1943, 1946–1950
Goose Goslin (outfielder) 1921–1938
Hank Greenberg (first baseman) 1930, 1933–1941, 1945–1947

Hall of Fame Players from the Golden Era (1925–1941)

Lefty Grove (pitcher) 1925–1941
Bucky Harris (player/manager) 1924–1943, 1947–1948, 1950–1956
Harry Hooper (outfielder) 1909–1925
Waite Hoyt (pitcher) 1918–1938
Miller Huggins (manager) 1913–1929
Walter Johnson (pitcher) 1907–1927
Tony Lazzeri (second baseman) 1926–1939
Bob Lemon (pitcher) 1941–1942, 1946–1958
Ted Lyons (pitcher) 1923–1942, 1946
Connie Mack (manager) 1894–1896, 1901–1950
Heinie Manush (outfielder) 1923–1939
Hal Newhouser (pitcher) 1939–1955
Herb Pennock (pitcher) 1912–1934
Sam Rice (outfielder) 1915–1934
Phil Rizzuto (shortstop) 1941–1942, 1946–1956
Red Ruffing (pitcher) 1924–1942, 1945–1947
Babe Ruth (outfielder) 1914–1935
Ray Schalk (catcher) 1912–1929
Joe Sewell (shortstop) 1920–1933
Al Simmons (outfielder) 1924–1944
George Sisler (first baseman) 1915–1922, 1924–1930
Tris Speaker (outfielder) 1907–1928
Ted Williams (outfielder) 1939–1942, 1946–1960
Early Wynn (pitcher) 1939, 1941–1944, 1946–1963

Chapter Notes

Chapter One

1. Norman L. Macht, Connie Mack and the Early Years of Baseball (Lincoln: University of Nebraska Press, 2007), p. 86.
2. Ibid., p. 131.
3. Warren N. Wilbert, The Arrival of the American League: Ban Johnson and the 1901 Challenge to National League Monopoly (Jefferson, NC: McFarland, 2007), p. 6.
4. Don Smith and Ed Croke, Professional Baseball: The First 100 Years (New York: Major League Baseball Promotional Corporation, 1969), p. 145, and St. John Daily Sun, January 29, 1901.
5. Bridgeport Herald, January 20, 1901.
6. Connie Mack, My 66 Years in the Big Leagues (Mineola, NY: Dover, 2009), pp. 28–29.
7. Ibid., p. 28.
8. Ibid.
9. "Nap Lajoie Was the Leader," Saskatoon Star-Phoenix, November 18, 1961.
10. Mack, p. 29.
11. Ibid., pp. 30–31.
12. Bruce Kuklick, To Everything a Season: Shibe Park and Urban Philadelphia 1909–1976 (Princeton: Princeton University Press, 1991), p. 28.
13. Mack, p. 32.
14. A.D. Suehsdorf, The Great American Baseball Scrapbook (New York: Random House, 1978), p. 56.
15. Mack, p. 36.

Chapter Two

1. Bill James, The Bill James Guide to Baseball Managers (New York: Scribner's, 1997), pp. 60–65.
2. David M. Jones, The Athletics of Philadelphia: Connie Mack's White Elephants, 1901–1954 (Jefferson, NC: McFarland, 1999), p. 90.
3. The Sporting News, June 6, 1935, p. 30.
4. Ruth Bear Levy, "Recollections of Lefty Grove: Baseball's Greatest Left-handed Pitcher, Part I," Maryland Historical Magazine, Summer 1987, p. 168.
5. Ruth Bear Levy, "Recollections of Lefty Grove: Baseball's Greatest Left-handed Pitcher, Part II," Maryland Historical Magazine, Summer 1988, p. 127.
6. Gordon S. Cochrane, Baseball: The Fan's Game (Cleveland: Society for American Baseball Research, 1992), p. 13.
7. James Duplacey and Joseph Romain, Baseball's Great Dynasties: The Athletics (New York: Gallery Books, 1991), pp. 13–14.
8. Levy, "Recollections," Pt. II, p. 129.
9. Ibid., p. 14.
10. Jordan, pp. 98–99.
11. Brett Topel, Simply the Best: The Story of the 1929–1931 Philadelphia Athletics (Charleston: Brett Topel, 2011), p. 26.
12. Ibid., pp. 18–19.
13. The Telegraph Herald and Times Journal, October 6, 1929, and The Toledo News Bee, October 2, 1929.
14. Topel, pp. 24–25.

15. Jim Kaplan, Lefty Grove: American Original (Cleveland: Society for American Baseball Research, 2000), p. 122, and Jordan, p. 103.
16. Levy, "Recollections," Pt. II, p. 129.

Chapter Three

1. Topel, p. 116.
2. Ibid., p. 109.
3. Ibid., pp. 59–60.
4. Kaplan, p. 43.
5. Ibid., pp. 44–45.
6. Ibid., pp. 46–48.
7. Jordan, p. 111.
8. Mack, p. 192.

Chapter Four

1. Kaplan, pp. 104, 144.
2. Norm Macht, Baseball Legends: Jimmie Foxx (New York: Chelsea House, 1991), pp. 30–33.

Chapter Five

1. Kaplan, p. 141.
2. Topel, p. 96.
3. Kaplan, p. 136.
4. Mack, p. 42.

Chapter Six

1. William Nack, "Lost in History," Sports Illustrated, August 19, 1996.
2. Kaplan, p. 137.
3. Ibid., pp. 110–111.
4. Ibid., p. 137.
5. Ibid., pp. 137, 145–146.
6. Ibid., pp. 150–151.

Chapter Seven

1. Topel, p. 119.

Chapter Eight

1. Ed Fitzgerald, The National League (New York: Grosset & Dunlap, 1966), pp. 190–191.

2. Ibid., p. 191.
3. Kaplan, p. 154.
4. Topel, p. 121.
5. Kaplan, p. 134.
6. Topel, p. 123.
7. Kaplan, p. 155.
8. Topel, p. 124.
9. The Sporting News, October 15, 1931.

Chapter Nine

1. Kaplan, p. 153.
2. Eric Morris, "Lefty's Shrine," Allegany Magazine 6, issue 3, 2011.
3. Kaplan, pp. 155–156.
4. Levy, "Recollections," Pt. II, p. 129.
5. Jordan, pp. 119–120.
6. Macht, Baseball Legends: Jimmie Foxx, p. 27, 41.
7. James Duplacey and Joseph Romain, Baseball's Great Dynasties: The Athletics (New York: Gallery Books, 1991), p. 18.
8. Ibid., p. 22.

Epilogue

1. William Nack, "Lost in History," Sports Illustrated, August 19, 1996.
2. Levy, "Recollections," Pt. II, p. 165.
3. Cumberland Times-News, December 10, 1961.
4. Letter from David Solosko to Carolyn Broadwater dated December 19, 2012.
5. Cumberland Times-News, May 25, 1975.
6. Kaplan, p. 263.
7. Ibid., p. 264.
8. Ibid., pp. 273–274.

Appendix 1

1. Levy, "Recollections," Pt. II, p. 139.

Bibliography

Newspapers, Magazines and Periodicals

Allegany Magazine
Bridgeport Herald
Cumberland Times-News
The Hardball Times
Maryland Historical Magazine
Philadelphia Evening Bulletin
Philadelphia Inquirer
Philadelphia Record
St. John Daily Sun
Saskatoon Star-Phoenix
The Sporting News
Sports Illustrated
The Telegraph Herald and Times Journal
The Toledo News Bee

Books

Cochrane, Gordon S. *Baseball: The Fan's Game*. Cleveland: Society for American Baseball Research, 1992.
Duplacey, James, and Joseph Romain. *Baseball's Great Dynasties: The Athletics*. New York: Gallery Books, 1991.
Dykes, Jimmie, and Charles O. Dexter. *You Can't Steal First Base*. Philadelphia: J.B. Lippincott, 1967.
Fitzgerald, Ed. *The National League*. New York: Grosset & Dunlap, 1966.
James, Bill. *The Bill James Guide to Baseball Managers*. New York: Scribner's, 1997.
Jordan, David M. *The Athletics of Philadelphia: Connie Mack's White Elephants 1901–1954*. Jefferson, NC: McFarland, 1999.
Kaplan, Jim. *Lefty Grove: American Original*. Cleveland: Society for American Baseball Research, 2000.
Kuklick, Bruce. *To Everything a Season: Shibe Park and Urban Philadelphia 1909–1976*. Princeton: Princeton University Press, 1991.
Lieb, Frederick G. *Connie Mack: Grand Old Man of Baseball*. New York: G.P. Putnam's Sons, 1945.

Bibliography

Macht, Norman L. *Connie Mack and the Early Years of Baseball*. Lincoln: University of Nebraska Press, 2007.

_____. *Jimmie Foxx*. New York: Chelsea House, 1991.

Mack, Connie. *My 66 Years in the Big Leagues*. Mineola, NY: Dover, 2009.

National Baseball Hall of Fame and Museum 2011 Yearbook. Lynn, MA: H.O. Zimman, 2011.

Sheed, Wilfrid. *My Life as a Fan*. New York: Simon & Schuster, 1993.

Smith, Don, and Ed Croke. *Professional Baseball: The First 100 Years*. New York: Major League Baseball Promotional Corporation, 1969.

Suehsdorf, A.D. *The Great American Baseball Scrapbook*. New York: Random House, 1978.

Topel, Brett. *Simply the Best: The Story of the 1929–1931 Philadelphia Athletics*. Charleston: Brett Topel, 2011.

Wilbert, Warren N. *The Arrival of the American League: Ban Johnson and the 1901 Challenge to National League Monopoly*. Jefferson, NC: McFarland, 2007.

Index

Adams, Sparky 141
Alexander, Dale 95
Alexander, Pete 171
Alou, Felipe 154
American League 1, 2, 5, 6, 7, 9, 10, 11, 12, 13, 14, 15, 16, 17, 18, 19, 29, 31, 43, 46, 48, 54, 59, 62, 57, 58, 70, 74, 76, 93, 113, 135, 148, 151, 166, 168
Andrews, Ivy 120, 123
Averill, Earl 86, 101, 112, 172

Baker, Frank "Home Run" 1, 17, 19, 20, 21, 26, 31
Bancroft, Dave 171
Bando, Sal 154, 155
Barry, Jack 17, 26
Bauer, Hank 153
Bender, Chief 1, 15, 16, 17, 18, 19, 20, 22, 24, 25, 157, 160, 172
Bernhard, Bill 13, 14
Bishop, Max 28, 31, 42, 44, 45, 46, 57, 79, 86, 95, 98, 99, 101, 103, 109, 110, 113, 114, 120, 121, 132, 136, 139, 141, 143, 146, 147, 151, 152, 168
Blades, Ray 45
Blaeholder, George 80, 104, 119
Blake, Sherriff 37, 41
Blue, Lu 98, 114
Blue Ridge League 53
Boley, Joe 40, 41, 61, 98, 99, 168
Boston Braves 22, 23, 24, 25, 160
Boston Red Sox 21, 30, 32, 54, 59, 65, 71, 72, 87, 90, 122, 123, 152
Bottomley, Jim 43, 45, 46, 136, 140, 141, 143, 171
Boudreau, Lou 172
Boyer, Clete 153
Braxton, Garland 73
Bridges, Tommy 65, 75, 83, 94, 130

Brown, Clint 63, 77, 83, 101, 127
Brown, Lloyd 56
Brown, Mordecai 18
Bucky Harris 173
Burke, Bobby 93
Burkett, Jesse 12
Burns, Jack 41, 76
Bush, Donie 97, 113, 114
Bush, Guy 37, 39, 40, 42
Bush, Joe 24, 25
Byrd, Sam 109

Campaneris, Bert 154
Caraway, Pat 62, 72, 78, 97, 99, 100, 115
Carey, Max 171
Carter, Sol 58, 170
Chance, Frank 18, 19
Chapman, Ben 68, 124
Chicago Cubs 6, 18, 37, 38, 39, 41, 161
Chicago White Sox 15, 26, 62, 72, 73, 78, 97, 98, 115, 150, 160
Cissell, Bill 98, 99, 113
Clemente, Roberto 3
Cleveland Indians 16, 32, 43, 63, 78, 84, 101, 112
Cobb, Ty 3, 5, 33, 34, 37, 170, 172
Cochrane, Mickey 1, 2, 5, 6, 7, 28, 30, 31, 33, 34, 36, 37, 39, 41, 42, 43, 46, 49, 51, 54, 59, 61, 62, 64, 65, 68, 75, 76, 85, 86, 88, 89, 99, 100, 101, 103, 104, 106, 107, 109, 112, 113, 120, 121, 122, 123, 124, 129, 132, 136, 137, 138, 139, 141, 143, 144, 145, 146, 147, 149, 151, 155, 159, 160, 151, 167, 168, 172
Coffman, Dick 76, 106, 116, 126
Collins, Eddie 1, 17, 18, 19, 21, 26, 32, 139, 160, 172
Columbia Park 13, 15, 17
Combs, Earle 33, 57, 68, 109, 110, 124, 172

179

Index

Comiskey, Charles 9, 11, 12
Connally, Sarge 103, 112
Coombs, Jack 18, 19, 20
Cramer, Doc 100, 104, 106, 109, 110, 112, 113, 121, 122, 126, 146, 168
Crandall, Doc 20
Cronin, Joe 57, 59, 172
Cross, Lave 13, 14
Crowder, General 56, 57, 88, 93, 107, 120, 121, 128
Cuccinello, Tony 151
Cuyler, Kiki 37, 39, 40, 171

Davis, Harry 13
Deal, Charlie 24
Demaree, Al 22
Den, Dizzy 171
Detroit Tigers 17, 65, 74, 75, 82, 94, 109, 111, 130, 151, 155, 160, 161
Dickey, Bill 2, 57, 68, 70, 109, 124, 133, 172
DiMaggio, Joe 172
Doerr, Bobby 172
Dolan, Joe 13
Doyle, Larry 20
Duggleby, Bill 14
Duncan, Dave 154
Dunn, Jack 30, 53
Durham, Ed 61, 65, 71, 72, 122, 132
Dykes, Jimmy 2, 28, 31, 36, 40, 41, 44, 45, 46, 64, 74, 79, 83, 86, 99, 110, 116, 120, 123, 129, 137, 142, 143, 144, 145, 146, 150, 151, 167

Earnshaw, George "Moose" 34, 36, 38, 39, 40, 43, 44, 46, 54, 56, 58, 59, 61, 62, 63, 65, 70, 71, 72, 73, 75, 77, 78, 81, 83, 88, 93, 94, 97, 100, 101, 105, 107, 108, 111, 120, 121, 122, 123, 125, 126, 127, 128, 129, 130, 131, 133, 135, 136, 139, 141, 145, 146, 155, 161, 169, 170
Ehmke, Howard 32, 33, 37, 38, 39, 41
English, Woody 40
Evers, Johnny 18, 23

Faber, Red 62, 73, 97, 113, 172
Feller, Bob 92, 165, 172
Fenway Park 21, 71
Ferrell Wes 63, 78, 102, 112, 128, 129
Fingers, Rollie 154, 156
Finley, Charles 153, 154
Fischer, Carl 58, 107
Flick, Elmer 12, 14

Flowers, Jake 139, 141, 144
Fonseca, Lew 98, 99, 113
Fothergill, Bob 113, 114
Foxx, Jimmie 1, 2, 6, 28, 30, 61, 32, 33, 34, 39, 40, 41, 42, 43, 44, 46, 48, 51, 54, 59, 61, 62, 65, 66, 67, 68, 75, 83, 86, 88, 89, 90, 98, 100, 101, 102, 103, 105, 107, 109, 112, 113, 115, 120, 121, 122, 124, 125, 129, 130, 139, 140, 141, 142, 143, 144, 145, 146, 149, 450, 151, 152, 155, 157, 159, 160, 162, 167, 168, 172
Fraser, Chick 13
Frazier, Vic 63, 79, 97, 100, 114
Frisch, Frankie 43, 45, 46, 134, 136, 137, 141, 142, 144, 149, 170, 171
Fultz, Dave 13

Gardner, Ethel 111
Gaston, Milt 72, 123
Gehrig, Lou 2, 5, 33, 49, 57, 68, 109, 110, 124, 133, 148, 149, 163, 170, 172
Gelbert, Charlie 45, 138, 140, 143
George's Creek Regional Library 149
Gomez, Lefty 49, 58, 70, 108, 120, 172
Gordon, Joe 172
Goslin, Goose 76, 81, 105, 106, 118, 119, 126, 172
Gowdy, Hank 25
Grandstaff, Richard 164
Gray, Sam 62, 77, 81, 106, 118, 126
Griffith Stadium 56, 88
Grimes, Burleigh 44, 46, 134, 136, 140, 141, 145, 146, 171
Grimm, Charlie 40
Grove, Robert M. "Lefty" 1, 2, 3, 4, 5, 6, 7, 28, 30, 31, 32, 33, 34, 36, 39, 43, 44, 45, 46, 51, 52, 53, 54, 56, 57, 58, 59, 62, 62, 63, 64, 65, 68, 70, 71, 72, 73, 74, 75, 76, 77, 78, 80, 82, 83, 87, 88, 92, 93, 95, 96, 102, 103, 105, 107, 109, 110, 111, 112, 113, 116, 117, 118, 120, 122, 125, 126, 128, 131, 132, 133, 135, 136, 137, 138, 140, 143, 144, 145, 147, 148, 149, 150, 151, 155, 156, 157, 159, 160, 162, 163, 164, 165, 166, 169, 172, 173
Grube, Frank 98, 113

Haas, George "Mule" 2, 24, 40, 41, 42, 44, 46, 58, 59, 61, 68, 75, 86, 89, 97, 99, 100, 103, 104, 106, 112, 129, 132, 136, 137, 144, 146, 150, 151, 168
Hadley, Bump 56, 58, 59, 88, 92, 93, 161

Index

Hafey, Chick 43, 45, 46, 134, 137, 140, 145, 171
Haines, Jesse 45, 134, 171
Hallahan, Bill 45, 46, 134, 135, 136, 139, 142, 143, 146, 147
Harris, Dave 93
Herbert, Walley 76, 80, 81, 105, 125
Herman, Billy 171
Herring, Art 82, 94, 111, 130
High, Andy 136, 138, 145, 146
Hogsett, Chief 130
Holtzman, Ken 155, 156
Hooper, Harry 21, 173
Hoover, Herbert 41
Hornsby, Rogers 3, 37, 39, 40, 170, 171
Hoyt, Waite 33, 74, 82, 87, 88, 90, 94, 100, 101, 104, 106, 107, 114, 118, 121, 122, 124, 126, 127, 129, 134, 135, 142, 169, 173
Hubbel, Carl 171
Hudlin, Willis 78, 86, 127
Huggins, Miller 33, 35
Hunter, Jim "Catfish" 154, 155, 156

Jackson, Reggie 154, 155, 156
Jackson, Travis 171
James, Bill 23, 24
Johnson, Arnold 152, 153
Johnson, Bancroft 9, 10, 11, 12
Johnson, Hank 58, 68, 108
Johnson, Roy 94
Johnson, Syl 46, 136, 138, 141, 142, 144
Jolley, Smead 129
Jones, Sam 27, 57, 106, 107, 121, 125

Kelley, George 171
Kelley, Joe 12
Kerr, John 48, 99, 113, 114
Killefer, Bill 80, 116
Killilea, Henry 9
Kimsey, Chad 80, 105
Klein, Chuck 171
Kline, Bob 72
Koenig, Mark 110
Krause, Eddie 18
Krause, Lew 86, 132, 170
Kremer, Ray 42
Kress, Red 105, 126
Kuhel, Joe 93
Kuhn, Bowie 166

Lajoie, Nap 12, 13, 14
Larson, Don 153

Lary, Lyn 109, 120, 124, 125
Lazzeri, Tony 33, 57, 109, 124, 173
League Park 77, 84, 104
Lemon, Bob 173
Levey, Jim 126
Lewis, Duffy 21
Lindsey, Jim 46, 142, 144, 145
Lindstrom, Fred 171
Lisenbee, Hod 72, 132
Lombardi, Ernie 171
Lopez, Hector 153
Lyons, Ted 73, 79, 173

MacFayden, Danny 122
Mack, Connie 1, 5, 9, 10, 13, 14, 15, 16, 17, 18, 20, 21, 25, 26, 27, 29, 30, 31, 33, 34, 36, 38, 39, 41, 42, 47, 48, 54, 55, 57, 58, 61, 62, 63, 65, 68, 71, 72, 74, 78, 82, 87, 89, 90, 91, 100, 105, 106, 108, 116, 117, 119, 120, 122, 124, 128, 129, 130, 131, 132, 135, 139, 141, 143, 145, 146, 147, 151, 152, 157, 159, 160, 161, 163, 173
MacPhail, Lee 166
Mahaffey, Roy 43, 58, 65, 71, 73, 76, 80, 83, 97, 90, 95, 99, 100, 101, 102, 108, 112, 115, 118, 119, 120, 121, 123, 124, 131, 135, 169
Malone, Pat 37, 41
Mancuso, Gus 138
Mann, Les 24
Manush, Heinie 173
Maranville, Rabbit 23, 149, 171
Marberry, Firpo 57, 88, 93, 106
Marcum, Johnny 152
Maris, Roger 153
Marquard, Rube 19, 21, 171
Martin, Billy 153
Martin, John "Pepper" 134, 137, 140, 141, 142, 143, 144, 145, 146, 147
Mathewson, Christy 19, 20, 21, 22, 148
McCarthy, Joe 108, 133
McDonald, Hank 57, 59, 72, 73, 77, 80, 81, 89, 90, 95, 98, 103, 106, 107, 124, 169
McGillicuddy, Cornelius *see* Connie Mack
McGinnis, Stuffy 17
McGraw, John 15, 16, 19, 21, 22, 23, 143, 171
McIntyre, Matty 13
McKain, Hal 73, 79, 100
McKechnie, Bill 171
McMillan, Norm 40
McNair, Eric 65, 101, 102, 104, 105, 109, 113, 125, 126, 128, 129, 168

Index

McNamee, Graham 44
McNeely, Earl 105
Medwick, Joe 171
Melillo, Ski 105, 116, 117
Miller, Bing 2, 28, 31, 36, 38, 39, 40, 42, 44, 61, 65, 72, 75, 86, 99, 100, 101, 102, 105, 107, 108, 113, 114, 120, 122, 137, 141, 142, 143, 144, 146, 167, 168
Miller, Jake 32, 63
Miller, Otis 131
Milwaukee Brewers 9, 10
Mize, Johnny 1471
Monday, Rick 154, 155
Montague, Ed 102, 128
Moore, Jim 100, 104, 105, 114, 115, 116, 117, 121, 122, 127, 128, 139
Moore, Wilcy 87, 90, 121, 123, 131
Moran, Herbie 25
Morris, Ed 72, 87, 90
Muesel, Bob 33
Mungo, Van 151
Musial, Stan 172

National League 1, 9, 10, 11, 12, 13, 15, 18, 21, 42, 117, 151
Navin Field 64, 83, 109
Nehf, Art 40, 41
New York Giants 15, 19, 20, 22
Newhouser, Hal 173

Odom, Johnny "Blue Moon" 154, 155, 156
Oldring, Rube 20
Oliver, Al 3
Orsatti, Ernie 146
Ott, Mel 170, 172

Palmisano, Joe 89, 130, 132
Peckinpaugh, Roger 102
Pennock, Herb 33, 58, 157, 160, 173
Perkins, Cy 30, 31
Peterman, Cy 51
Peterson, Jim 94, 124, 130
Pipgras, George 70, 108
Pittsburgh Pirates 3, 4, 42, 140
Plank, Eddie 1, 13, 14, 15, 16, 17, 18, 19, 21, 22, 24, 25
Player's League 9

Quinn, Jack 33, 40

Reese, Jimmie 90
Reese, Pee Wee 171

Reynolds, Carl 98, 113, 114
Rhodes, Gordon 124
Rinker, F. Blaine 165
Rixey, Eppa 172
Robinson, Wilbert 172
Roettger, Wally 136, 138, 141, 144
Rommel, Eddie 40, 58, 62, 63, 70, 72, 80, 81, 97, 104, 107, 119, 120, 123, 124, 127, 130, 169
Root, Charlie 37, 38, 39, 40
Roush, Eddie 172
Rudi, Joe 154
Rudolph, Dick 23, 24, 25
Ruffing, Red 57, 65, 89, 90, 108
Russell, Jack 62, 71, 122
Ruth, Babe 2, 3, 5, 6, 33, 37, 48, 57, 58, 68, 108, 109, 110, 120, 124, 125, 162, 163, 170, 173

St. Louis Browns 15, 36, 59, 62, 76, 80, 89, 119, 125
St. Louis Cardinals 6, 43, 44, 133, 134
Schalk, Ray 173
Seeds, Bob 102
Sewell, Joe 54, 109, 124, 173
Seybold, Socks 13
Shawkey, Bob 25
Shibe, Benjamin 13, 14, 16, 17, 18, 27
Shibe Park 16, 18, 19, 22, 24, 32, 39, 41, 44, 46, 56, 59, 68, 72, 75, 76, 87, 91, 95, 97, 107, 117, 121, 125, 128, 151, 152
Shores, Bill 77, 79, 81, 170
Simmons, Al 1, 6, 7, 28, 31, 32, 33, 34, 38, 41, 42, 43, 44, 45, 46, 49, 50, 54, 57, 61, 68, 86, 88, 89, 90, 93, 95, 99, 100, 101, 102, 104, 105, 107, 108, 109, 110, 111, 112, 117, 118, 125, 128, 129, 132, 134, 137, 138, 141, 142, 143, 145, 146, 149, 150, 155, 157, 159, 160, 161, 157, 173
Sisler, George 173
Slaughter, Enos 172
Smith, Ken 164
Solosko, David 164
Sorrell, Vic 75, 95, 109
Sorti, Lin 106
Southworth, Billy 172
Speaker, Tris 21, 34, 170, 173
Speece, By 32
Stargell, Willie 3
Stengel, Casey 172
Stephenson, Riggs 37
Stewart, Lefty 76, 77, 81, 105, 118, 119

Index

Stiles, Rollie 80
Stone, John 95
Street, Charles "Gabby" 134, 135, 136, 142, 146
Stumpf, George 131
Sullivan, Billy, Jr. 67, 98, 114, 115, 128
Sullivan, Charlie 95, 109
Sweeney, Bill 131

Tate, Bennie 114
Tenace, Gene 154, 156
Terry, Bill 172
Terry Park Ballfield 48
Tesreau, Jeff 22
Thomas, Tommy 62, 73, 79, 97, 98, 99, 111, 113
Tinker, Joe 18
Todt, Phil 58, 103, 107, 121, 122, 126, 127
Traynor, Pie 172
Tyler, Lefty 23, 24

Uhle, George 32, 64, 83, 95, 111, 130

Vance, Dazzy 151, 172
Vosmik, Joe 102

Waddell, George E. "Rube" 1, 10, 14, 15, 16
Walberg, Rube 28, 33, 37, 39, 40, 41, 45, 54, 56, 59, 62, 64, 65, 67, 71, 72, 74, 75, 76, 78, 80, 81, 83, 86, 88, 93, 97, 101, 103, 104, 106, 109, 111, 112, 114, 115, 119, 120, 123, 125, 127, 129, 133, 135, 143, 146, 151, 152, 155, 169, 170
Walker, Luke 3
Wallace, Bobby 12
Waner, Lloyd 172
Waner, Paul 172
Washington Senators 21, 31, 48, 54, 56, 92, 93, 107, 121, 160
Watwood, Johnny 98, 99, 129
Webb, Earl 61, 90, 131
Wells, Ed 58
Western League 9, 10, 11
Wheat, Zack 33, 34, 172
Whitehill, Earl 75, 95, 111
Williams, Ted 166, 173
Wilson, Hack 37, 39, 40, 41, 172
Wood, Smokey Joe 112
Wrigley Field 38
Wynn, Early 173

Yawkey, Tom 163
Youngs, Ross 172
Yowell, Carl 32

www.ingramcontent.com/pod-product-compliance
Ingram Content Group UK Ltd.
Pitfield, Milton Keynes, MK11 3LW, UK
UKHW042014140426
5217IPUK00015B/1161